The Richardson Cancer Prevention Diet

Other Books by Dr. Janet Starr Hull

Sweet Poison: How the World's Most Popular Artificial Sweetener
       Is Killing Us – My Story
10 Steps To Detoxification
Splenda: Is It Safe or Not?

Visit Dr. Hull's website and sign up for her free health newsletter:

http://www.janethull.com

Also visit Dr. Hull's alternative cancer diet websites for updates, news,
and more.

http://www.alternativecancerdiet.com
http://www.richardsoncancerdiet.com

THE RICHARDSON CANCER PREVENTION DIET

By
Janet Starr Hull, PhD, CN

The Pickle Press
Dallas, Texas

Hull, Janet Starr
 The Richardson Cancer Prevention Diet

ISBN: 0-9771843-2-3

Jacket Cover: Alex Egner
http://www.eggnerd.com

Jacket Photo: Pawel Roslek
http://www.istockphoto.com

The Pickle Press
http://www.thepicklepress.com
Manufactured in the U.S.A.

Disclaimer

This book is based on my personal experiences and research, and reflects my perceptions of the past, present and future. All information presented in this book is the result of my personal research and collaboration with professional, academic, and government colleagues, internationally. The personalities, events, actions, and conversations portrayed within the book have been reconstructed from my memory, various legal records, letters, personal papers, and press accounts. Some names and events have been altered to protect the privacy of individuals. Events involving the characters happened as described; only minor details have been altered.

This book is for educational purposes only and not intended to be considered legal, medical, or any other professional service. The information provided is not a replacement for professional advice or care. If you require nutritional, medical, or other expert services, please seek appropriate professional care. The author, contributors, publisher and their employees are not liable or held accountable for any damages arising from or in association with the application of any information contained in this book.

Acknowledgements

Many thanks to Dr. Steve Richardson, Dr. John Richardson's son, for his contribution to the book and his permission to share his father's heartfelt work and dedication to health and wellness.

To Andy Smith, Founder of the Pickle Network and the Pickle Press, for making this book available to everyone on the Internet – and beyond.

Table Of Contents

Author's Note

"To unlock the doors of future health,
we MUST find the keys from the past."
– Janet Hull

Modern medicine has led human beings to the "take a pill" or "cut it out" mentality for almost every modern health symptom, but these approaches do not cure disease, as more and more people are personally discovering. If anything, we just keep getting sicker and more physically tired until our bodies eventually give in to disease. Curing cancer and degenerative diseases as in times past might be considered old-fashioned and outdated when compared to today's high tech standards, but our physical bodies have neither changed over time nor have the effects of disease, just the magnitude of modern treatments and the chemicals that cause illness. We must not forget the roots of disease and their cures are as old-fashioned as the body itself. I cured myself of a diagnosed "incurable" case of Grave's Disease using old-fashioned nutritional techniques, refusing to buy into the exclusivity of the modern-day medical system.

Humans, along with other animals, are becoming diseased waste sites for manmade chemicals and artificial food additives. That's a harsh statement, but cancer rates in the United States are among the highest in the world, and association with medical doctors represents the third leading cause of death in the United States through unnecessary surgeries, over-medication and medication errors in hospitals, infections in hospitals, and negative effects of drugs.

It's important to remember the human body has not "kept up" with modern technology. Human beings certainly shouldn't eat technology! But that is happening today as a result of the onslaught of manufactured foods, more and more chemicals being pumped into our societies, and the threat of chemical warfare. This very second, your physical body is, without our understanding, functioning internally exactly the way human bodies functioned 10,000 years ago. Because our bodies today are the same as in the past, it is critical to treat them the same as in years past - centuries past. But, human beings are adopting one of the most unnatural lifestyles known to mankind and are becoming diseased because of it.

Finding nutritional answers to illness is an art passed down from generation to generation. The causes of modern diseases are harder to identify today than ever before, and the various sources of high-tech diseases have become lost in today's technological shuffle. As time marches forward, too much information is forgotten. We must reclaim past healing techniques.

I learned, through my own illness, that curing a physical ailment can be very challenging. Do your research; study all you can about your disease and the alternatives that are available to you. Nutrition is an important part of healing from any illness.

Dr. Richardson's approach to treating cancer turns back time, reviving the fundamentals of what nutrition and natural medicine used to be before the dependence on insanely expensive pharmaceuticals dominated our lives. Sharing his life's work, Dr. Richardson illustrated how cancer and many other degenerative diseases can be prevented and treated using nutrition and proper vitamin and mineral supplementation.

I am by no means advising you to go against your doctor's counsel, but I am sharing with you some very important nutritional information doctors used many years ago, but do not practice today. The research and recommendations within this book will serve as a base to enrich your knowledge.

To Your Health!

Janet Hull

Prologue

June 2, 1972: 10:00 A.M. Without warning, two police cars followed by two unmarked government vehicles screeched to a halt in front of an unsuspecting medical clinic in California. Uniformed officers surrounded the building and with guns drawn, as if ordered to kill, ten police officers burst through the front door of the quiet clinic. They boldly flashed an intimidating search warrant at the stunned young receptionist and pushed their way into the recently painted halls of the worn-out infirmary. With his stethoscope swinging like the pendulum of an antique mahogany clock, Dr. John Richardson, M.D. was ambushed, thrust against a wall and frisked for a concealed weapon. Horrified, the nurses were confined to their stations as if each were guilty of committing a crime. The patients, with one exception, were ordered by the uniformed officers to go home without protest.

Dr. Richardson was immediately placed under arrest for violating the California "Anti-Quackery" Law. He had been administering vitamin B17 to his cancer patients, a natural cyanide-containing compound also known as Laetrile. All Laetrile and any literature pertaining to it were militantly confiscated. By this time, California Health Department agents were swarming everywhere like ants on a cookie crumb; flinging open cupboards, violently pulling out drawers, savagely tearing apart the contents of closets, and hurriedly examining books in the medical library for hollowed-out secret compartments.

Dazed, Dr. Richardson refused to answer any of the questions fired at him until he called his attorney. He was denied the request. Rattled, he asked to call his wife at home. He was denied again. Deprived of alternatives, he sat in silence as the frenetic agents rummaged through every drawer and shelf at his disheveled clinic.

During the raid, seven-year-old Kerry Alderson sat motionless in one of the examination rooms awaiting cancer treatment. She had recently begun metabolic therapy for an advanced case of bone cancer. When she first came to Dr. Richardson's clinic, he didn't think she had much chance of survival. They had discovered the cancer too late, and conventional cancer treatments were not working. Dr. Richardson had earnestly discussed his medical opinion about the case with Kerry's parents, telling them he was willing to do everything possible for her. Her medical doctors had given up on her, advising her parents there was nothing more they could do for their daughter.

Kerry responded beautifully to the Laetrile cancer treatments. Her appetite increased and she began regaining much of the weight she had lost during her illness. She had gratifying freedom from pain and "smiled for the first time in months" according to her parents. One of her legs had continued to fester and swell, nonetheless, and Dr. Richardson was very worried about her chances of complete recovery.

As a result of the raid, Dr. Richardson was not able to treat Kerry as scheduled. Normally, she would have received a massive injection of vitamins, including vitamin B17. Her scheduled treatment would have relieved the pain and swelling. With armed guards standing watch, Dr. Richardson was only allowed to clean and dress her lesions before sending her home. It was evident to Dr. Richardson that Kerry and her parents were extremely upset by the raid and the militant intrusion of the unwelcome police officers.

After Dr. Richardson sent Kerry home, he was immediately arrested, handcuffed, ruthlessly marched out the front door of his clinic, pushed into a police car, and hauled off to jail.

PROLOGUE

Kerry died three days later.

CHAPTER 1

The Richardson Cancer Prevention Diet

"First do no harm."
- Hippocrates

Ifirst learned of Dr. Richardson's cancer diet from the nutritionist who helped me cure my Grave's Disease in 1991. After reading the cancer case histories in his journals, I noted that the Richardson Diet was referenced quite often. I decided to locate the original research from which Dr. Richardson gained his medical knowledge, while exploring the Richardson Diet further. After digging through a number of esteemed vintage medical journals, I finally uncovered the rare original documents outlining Dr. Richardson's dietary plan. I was not only healing my own incurable disease at this time, but was simultaneously rediscovering medical history.

According to Dr. Richardson, the medical regimen he adopted was a very natural and humane approach to treating cancer. Adopted from the records of medical researchers from the turn of centuries past, Dr. Richardson's clinic reflected the philosophy of Hippocrates, the Father of Medicine, who taught his students, "First do no harm."

Dr. Richardson's Diet

1.   THE DIET:
     Principally eat:
     • Fresh fruits
     • Vegetables

- Seeds
- Nuts
- Grains

All animal protein, including dairy products, should be excluded during cancer recovery.

2. TOBACCO, ALCOHOL, and COFFEE:
- Not to be used at all.

3. VITAMIN B17 (LAETRILE OR AMYGDALIN) TABLETS:
- One (1) to four (4) 500-milligram tablets recommended to be taken on the days the patient does not receive the vitamin through injection.
- Two (2) Laetrile tablets per day recommended during the first year.
- Most of Dr. Richardson's patients continued the tablets for the remainder of their lives.
- Some patients took only 100-milligram tablets and supplemented their daily intake with apricot kernels rich in natural B17. The kernels were taken opposite days from the vitamin B17 tablets.
- Note: Laetrile injections and tablets are currently unlawful in the United States, but can be administered legally in other countries.

4. PANCREATIC ENZYMES:
- Two (2) to four (4) milligram tablets recommended four times daily.

The pancreatic enzymes assist the body in the digestion of all protein, especially animal protein. They function in the intestines and in the blood, aiding digestion specifically in the intestines.

5. VITAMIN B15 (PANGAMIC ACID):
- Fifty (50) milligrams recommended three times daily. (B15 is also currently outlawed in the United States.)

6. VITAMIN C:
    - 750 milligrams to 2,000 milligrams of ascorbic acid (not from corn) to be taken initially by the patient daily. Increase to bowel tolerance.
    - An individual can determine their daily need by the texture of their stools. When vitamin C is 100 percent cellular saturation, a loose stool will occur.

7. AMINO ACID TABLETS:
    - Three (3) to nine (9) tablets required daily to compensate for the reduced intake of mineral protein.

8. CHELATED MINERALS:
    - Recommended at a dosage dependent upon the type and extent of deficiency revealed by a mineral hair analysis.

9. THERAPEUTIC VITAMINS AND MINERALS:
    - Supplemented with one (1) to two (2) capsules daily.

10. VITAMIN E:
    - 800 I.U. to 1,200 I.U. recommended daily.

11. LIQUID PROTEIN: (if not using amino acid tablets regularly)
    - Supplemented two (2) to four (4) teaspoons daily.
    - This liquid protein to be in predigested form to provide the basic amino acids but not requiring pancreatic enzymes for deployment.
    - Those not using the amino acid tablets were asked to use the liquid protein.

    Note: The amino acid supplement should contain all the essential amino acids combined, not in individual or isolated form. This is an important point because in nature, amino acids are intended to work together. Manufacturing has isolated the amino acids but as with all other animals, they are to be eaten naturally in conjunction with one another.

12. ADDITIONAL VITAMINS AND MINERALS:
- Recommended per individual.

* * *

Not every one of Dr. Richardson's cancer cases had an unhappy ending like Kerry's. There were many success stories. In April of 1967, Shane Horton, Richardson's case #150, was six years old when he developed bone cancer of the right upper arm and of the spine. The cancer was confirmed both by X-ray and bone marrow biopsy. Orthodox doctors advised Shane's parents there was no hope for Shane's recovery. It was at this point when his parents elected to try B17 therapy.

Three years after Shane began B17 therapy, all evidence of bone cancer vanished. Shane was enjoying the life of a completely normal nine-year-old boy. Shane's health had restored.

Dr. Richardson's innovative view on cancer is an inspiring one. He identified cancer as a nutritional deficiency of vitamin B17, pancreatic enzymes, or both. Quite simply, Dr. Richardson began seeing positive recovery results in cancer patients like Shane when B17, pancreatic enzymes, vitamin C, and multi-vitamin and mineral supplements were administered to them.

Dr. Richardson's patients did not generally experience the side effects from Laetrile and B17 treatments that were common to orthodox cancer treatments - side effects such as:
- Undesirable loss of hair
- Severe vomiting
- Diarrhea
- Debilitating dizziness

His patients reported:
- A welcome reduction in pain
- A healthy increase of appetite
- A gradual return of strength
- A drastic improvement in their mental outlook
- Hypertensive (high blood pressure) patients showed a marked return to normal blood pressure after vitamin treatments

Traditional medical doctors had previously diagnosed many of Dr. Richardson's patients with "terminal" cases of cancer. Like Kerry, they came to Dr. Richardson as a last resort, hoping for a healing miracle. Many ultimately passed away, but at least they acquired a release from pain, their human dignity was restored (many of them having body parts permanently removed in previous surgeries), they experienced an extension of their lives not expected by orthodox medical and pharmaceutical communities, and their personal quality of life was improved.

Dr. Richardson was not a lumps-and-bumps cancer doctor. He subjectively defined cancer as a systemic condition, interpreting the lumps-and-bumps as symptoms of a much larger condition, not the disease itself.

As defined by Dr. Richardson, malignant tumors are a mixture of cancer tissue cells and non-cancer tissue cells. The average tumor has a greater portion of non-cancerous tissue as opposed to cancerous tissue. The tumor may actually be a natural part of the body's defense system fighting *against* the cancer. In other words, instead of fearing a tumor, patients can actually be relieved to see its appearance.

According to Dr. Richardson, when cancer begins to form, the body surrounds the cancerous cells with millions of non-cancerous cells in an apparent effort to seal off the cancer; isolating it in the same way the body surrounds and seals a simple splinter. The tumor actually attempts to protect the body from the spread of cancerous cells. If the body's pancreatic factors, known as enzymes, and the vitamin and mineral levels are adequate, according to Dr. Richardson the immune system can actually keep cancerous cells in check. If this "air-tight seal" surrounding the lump or bump is broken by cutting into it or invading it with radiation, there is a chance the body's own natural barrier will be destroyed, recklessly spreading the disease throughout the body.

If a cancerous tumor grows without therapy to aid the healthy cells in fighting the cancerous cells inside it, the life of the host is obviously threatened. Dr. Richardson's revolutionary ideas were never designed to jeopardize the health of his patients, only to rebuild their natural defense systems to fight the cancer from the inside out. He never stopped believing that it is not the cancer that kills, but the breakdown of the body's own defense mechanism that brings death. Every cancer patient he witnessed working hard to stay healthy actually boosted their level of health enough to rebuild their own natural resistance, thereby increasing their chances to fight their cancer.

"Instead of patients spending their final days or years butchered in surgical theaters or microwaved in chemotherapy and radiation rooms," Dr. Richardson wrote in 1977, "I have witnessed my patients experiencing an improved quality of life and enjoyment in their remaining time."

John Richardson always believed orthodox medicine looked only at the lumps-and-bumps of cancer as the "total cancer." But he could not convince the State of California, the state in which he held his medical license, to agree with his insightful philosophy. It was at this time that the State of California passed the Anti-Quackery Law, a law stating that cancer was *a space-occupying lesion only, and any therapy that does not attack that lesion was, by definition, 'quackery.'* The law also decreed that anyone who did not conform to these opinions was subject to criminal prosecution.

That's exactly what happened to Dr. John Richardson of Albany, California. He faced more legal harassment from state authorities than any other practicing physician at the time. His medical license was indefinitely suspended, he was arrested twice more, and was forced to stand trial four times for using vitamin B17 in his medical practice. By 1977, he had spent more than six exasperating months defending himself in unsympathetic courtrooms. In his fourth and final trial, the state finally succeeded in securing a conviction against him. The State of California ultimately spent thousands of dollars destroying Dr. Richardson's preeminent medical practice and livelihood, along with his patients' hopes.

Prosecution by the state finally prohibited the use of vitamin B17 in cancer therapy and claimed justification for this law based on two assumptions:

1. Vitamin B17 was "unproven" in the cure for cancer
2. Orthodox therapies - surgery, radiation, and chemotherapy - were to be considered the only "proven" cures, offering the patient an excellent chance of recovery if started in time

Cancer treatments using nutritional supplements, particularly vitamin B17, were presumed worthless and unlawful primarily because they prevented the particular patient from obtaining exclusive orthodox cancer treatment.

WHAT IS B17?

According to research provided by nutritionists and medical scientists from years past, vitamin B17 is a natural cyanide-containing compound that gives up its cyanide content only in the presence of a particular enzyme group called beta glucosidase or glucuronidase. Miraculously, this enzyme group is found almost exclusively in cancer tissue. If found elsewhere, it is accompanied by greater quantities of another enzyme, rhodanese, which has the ability to disable the cyanide and convert it into completely harmless substances. Cancer tissues do not have this protecting enzyme. Therefore, cancer cells are faced with a double threat: the presence of one enzyme exposing them to cyanide, while the absence of another enzyme found in all other normal cells results in the cancer's failure to detoxify itself. Leave it to nature: the cyanide destroys the cancer cell. The cancer cells that are unable to withstand the cyanide are destroyed. The non-cancerous cells are not threatened by the cyanide and remain unharmed. I never underestimate the body's potential.

Vitamin B17 is found _naturally_ in many foods. If you eat foods containing vitamin B17, your body will know what to do next. All other animals in nature instinctively do this. Consider it nature's cancer prevention. If only modern medicine would allow it.

San Francisco's Ernst T. Krebs, Sr., M.D. discovered the healing qualities of vitamin B17 in 1923. His sons, Ernst T. Krebs, Jr., PhD., and Byron Krebs, M.D. continued their father's research, refining Laetrile's B17 healing qualities in 1952.

The Krebs' theory was the basis for Dr. Richardson's practice. The Krebs believed that cancer was not caused by an outside invading force but rather by malfunctions of the normal mechanics within the body itself. The malfunctions were the result of a deficiency of certain chemicals found in food, a deficiency of chemicals they identified as vitamin B17, as well as a deficiency of enzymes known as trypsins produced in the pancreas. These were the reasons Drs. Richardson and Krebs identified cancer as a "deficiency disease."

Vitamin B17 is also referred to as a "nitriloside," which is the foundation for Laetrile, amygdalin, and prunasin. Together, with the pancreatic enzyme trypsin, these can form a natural barrier against cancer growth. If foods containing any of the nitrilosides are eaten regularly, the body's own immune mechanisms can battle cancer-forming cells naturally. But if foods containing these critical vitamins are not regularly consumed, nature's mechanisms can't work as effectively against the buildup of factors at the root of cancer and the countless number of degenerative diseases.

This is happening to human beings today. Not only are advanced societies environmentally polluted to dangerous levels, but also many foods have been altered by man from their natural state. Modern freeze-dried, fat-free, sugar-free, calorie-free, weight-watchful, micro-wavable artificial food substitutes don't contain nitrilosides. Most food manufacturers don't even know what nitrilosides are. Never in human history have artificial foods saturated with preservatives and unhealthy chemicals dominated the food supply to the degree they do today. Modern nourishment is no longer nourishing.

The Krebs discovered a natural drugless method to fight cancer. But their discovery wasn't original, merely rediscovered from many years before their father's findings. Drs. George B. Wood and Franklin Bache, M.D. published a reference volume in **1833** in which they described amygdalin, derived from B17, as a common treatment for a wide range of diseases and disorders.

Dr. Richardson believed in the Krebs' rediscovery and put it to practice. However, he had no idea what was in store for him when he ordered his first supply of amygdalin derived from B17.

Dr. Richardson's first patient to receive Laetrile was the sister of one of his nurses. She had an advanced malignant melanoma on her left arm. Her attending physician told her she had about six weeks to live. They could slow the spread of the cancer if they immediately ampu-tated her arm, but she was told this would not save her life.

The woman came to Dr. Richardson for help. He administered the B17 Laetrile, and the lesions on her arm immediately began to heal. Within two months her arm returned to normal. She was put on a maintenance program, taking daily oral dosages of the vitamin-rich Laetrile. This occurred in the summer of 1971. As of 1977, she was still alive and doing well. If she reduced her dosage of the Laetrile, however, hair began to grow on the former cancerous site and her arm swelled. The symptoms retreated with the return of the recommend-ed level of Laetrile. She also received an unexpected bonus from the vitamin therapy. She had been an insulin-dependent diabetic and was eventually able to discontinue her use of insulin after adopting the Richardson Diet and maintaining the recommended doses of Laetrile. (I recommend checking with your medical doctor before ever decreasing insulin, and decreasing insulin should always be done in stages.)

When the woman later returned to her orthodox doctor for a routine check-up, the doctor was astonished that her cancer was gone. He still wanted to amputate her arm. She asked the doctor in awe, "Would you recommend amputation if you had never seen me before?"

"No," he answered, his voice cracking. "But because I saw your cancer, I believe that amputation is the only safe and sensible course of action to take."

Well, she didn't follow his advice. Did he think she really would? Throwing back both her arms proudly, the woman stood up as if called to attention and curtly walked out of the doctor's plush office, never to return again.

CHAPTER 2

Cancer Prevention Tools

VITAMINS B15 AND B17

Americans cannot access vitamins B15 or B17 because the FDA has taken these two vitamins off the market. It is unlawful for any health practitioner to administer these vitamins to their patients today. These two vitamins, along with apricot seeds (the best source for B17) have been taken off the shelves in every health food store throughout the US. Only limited research has been conducted on vitamin B17 since 1977 because of this impounding.

So, exactly what are these two vitamins and how are they helpful in cancer recovery?

VITAMIN B15

Vitamin B15 is also known as Pangamic Acid. The FDA has been monitoring the wide range of medical conditions treated with B15 in other countries.

The Soviet Union has been the most progressive about B15, feeling that it is a very important nutrient with physiological actions that can treat a multitude of symptoms and diseases. Soviet scientists have shown that Pangamic Acid supplementation can reduce the buildup of lactic acid in athletes and thereby lessen muscle fatigue and increase endurance. It is used regularly in Russia for many health problems, including:

- Alcoholism
- Drug addiction
- Aging and senility
- Minimal brain damage in children
- Autism
- Schizophrenia
- Heart disease
- High blood pressure
- Diabetes
- Skin diseases
- Liver disease
- Chemical poisonings

Dimethyl glycine (DMG) is used in the United States as a substitute for outlawed B15 as it is believed to enhance natural Pangamic Acid production in the body. Dimethyl glycine combines with gluconic acid to form Pangamic Acid, and DMG is an active component of Pangamic Acid.

Pangamic Acid is found in:
- Whole grains such as brown rice
- Brewer's yeast
- Pumpkin and sunflower seeds
- Apricot kernels
- Beef blood

B15 helps in the formation of certain amino acids such as methionine. It plays a role in the oxidation of glucose in cell respiration. Like vitamin E, it acts as an antioxidant helping to lengthen cell life through its protection from oxidation. Pangamic Acid mildly stimulates the endocrine and nervous systems, and by enhancing liver function, it helps in the detoxification process.

B15 has been shown to lower blood cholesterol and improve circulation and general oxygenation of cells and tissues. It is helpful for arteriosclerosis and hypertension, two of America's most common diseases.

In Europe, vitamin B15 has been used to treat premature aging because of both its circulatory stimulation and its antioxidant effect. It protects the body from pollutants, especially carbon monoxide. Pangamic Acid (and DMG) offers support for anyone living in a large polluted city or under high stress.

In Russia, Pangamic Acid is used in treating alcohol dependency and in reducing alcohol cravings. It has been reported to diminish a hangover. B15 has also been used to treat fatigue, as well as asthma and rheumatism, and even possesses some antiallergenic properties.

Some child psychiatrists have reported good results using Pangamic Acid with emotionally disturbed children, as it seems to stimulate speaking ability and other mental functions. In other countries, B15 is a nutritional prospect to aid in autism, but more research is needed.

It is currently illegal to distribute B15 in the United States, though it was used as a supplement for some time through the 1970s. The most common form of Pangamic Acid, was at one time, calcium pangamate, but currently it is dimethyl glycine (DMG), which is the active component that has been hailed in the Soviet Union.

Pangamic Acid (or DMG) is often taken with vitamin E and vitamin A. A common amount of DMG is 50–100 mg. taken twice daily, usually with breakfast and dinner. This level of intake may improve general energy levels, support the immune system, and is also thought to reduce cravings for alcohol and thus may be very helpful in moderating chronic alcohol problems.

MORE ABOUT VITAMIN B17

In the late 1970's, Dr. Harold W. Manner, PhD., Chairman of the Biology Department at Loyola University, Chicago, Illinois, studied the overall value of Laetrile. His work was well respected and considered to be among the first unbiased studies since the Krebs' discovery in the 1920s. He reported Laetrile as being virtually non-toxic. When Dr. Manner used Laetrile along with vitamin A and digestive enzymes, the production of antibodies was stimulated against spontaneous breast tumors in his laboratory mice. He studied the results of complete regression in 76 percent of the treated mice with mammary gland cancers.

As Dr. Richardson and the Krebs before him did, Dr. Manner believed Laetrile received its best results when used in conjunction with digestive enzymes, a traditional balanced diet, vitamin A, and other natural vitamin and mineral supplements.

No physician has had more clinical experience with Laetrile than Ernesto Contreras, Sr., M.D. of the Contreras Hospital in Tijuana, Mexico, formerly The Oasis Of Hope Hospital. Dr. Contreras has clinically used Laetrile for more than 40 years on thousands of terminally-diagnosed patients and has received impressive results.

One of Dr. Contreras' patients was a man suffering from severe colon cancer. Using Laetrile alone, Contreras was able to arrest his patient's cancer. The man lived more than 15 years beyond his predicted death.

The following is a list of foods rich in vitamin B17:
- Watercress
- Spinach
- Bamboo sprouts
- Alfalfa sprouts
- Lentil sprouts
- Whole nuts

- Mung bean sprouts
- Ground nuts
- Garbanzo sprouts
- Apple seeds
- Apricot seeds

While researching Dr. Richardson's diet, the importance of "enzymes" was constantly stressed. I decided to probe further into what digestive enzymes are and how they aid in the B17 cancer diet.

THE IMPORTANCE OF ENZYMES

I discovered that enzyme therapy is an important and critical step in restoring health. Enzymes help to remedy digestive problems and are crucial in the elimination of all toxins from the body, including toxins released by cancer itself. If not eliminated properly, toxins build and worsen the condition.

PLANT ENZYMES

Plant enzymes and pancreatic enzymes are used to improve digestion and to aid in the absorption of essential nutrients. They are found naturally in a healthy whole foods diet. Enzymes are the "substances that make life possible." No vitamin, mineral, or hormone can function without the presence of enzymes. Enzymes literally "build" the body using proteins, carbohydrates, and fats. Without the aid of enzymes, the body cannot properly utilize any required nutrients.

Plant enzymes stimulate the digestive system. Pancreatic enzymes work for proper function of both the digestive system and the immune system. With proper digestion, which includes efficient elimination, many acute and chronic conditions may be prevented all together.

From my own disease recovery, I experienced first hand that enzymes are critical to good health and virtual elimination of disease. I never realized how critical until I witnessed their effects for myself.

The human body manufactures approximately 20 different digestive enzymes. These enzymes digest protein, carbohydrates, sugars, and fats. When you eat, you digest your food in stages. Digestion begins in the mouth. This is one reason why you shouldn't drink during a meal; the fluid washes away the initial digestive enzymes. Digestion then moves into the stomach, and finally passes through the small intestine. During each stage of digestion, specific enzymes break down the different types of foods.

This digestive process remains miraculously balanced throughout the body. At each point along the way, a different degree of acidity determines which enzymes function while others are not needed. Your body knows exactly what to do and when to do it, given the right tools - tools such as natural foods saturated with enzymes.

Plant enzymes are derived from the plants you eat. They can also be supplied through natural supplements, which only substitute those enzymes found naturally in food. Ideally, eat your enzymes, but if you aren't eating enough enzymes, supplement with the natural plant enzymes themselves.

Plant enzymes become active in the mouth and in the stomach. Fresh fruits, vegetables, nuts, and seeds provide plentiful plant enzymes. Eating raw foods or supplementing food enzymes can aid in 30 percent of the protein digestion and help digest 10 percent of the fat you eat in less than one hour. The body knows what to do.

Cooking destroys plant enzymes. Plant enzymes are more heat sensitive than vitamins. They are the first to be destroyed above 118 degrees Fahrenheit.

Proper chewing of food also helps enzymes begin immediate digestion. Chewing liberates cellulase, one of the plant enzymes found in food. If you don't chew properly, the cellulase is never released. Cellulase may also be lacking in packaged foods because of processing. Some supermarkets and salad bars spray fresh fruits and vegetables with chemicals that destroy the cellulase enzyme. Carryout and fast foods contain no cellulase.

Pancreatic Enzymes

Pancreatic enzymes are animal-derived enzymes that work hard in the intestines and within the blood. Amylase is a pancreatic enzyme. Enzyme supplements aid digestion in the intestines by sharing the workload of the body's own pancreatic enzymes active there. They do not, however, work in the stomach, the domain of the plant enzymes. If plant enzymes are not adequately digesting your food in the stomach, pancreatic enzymes pick up the extra workload, adding stress to the intestines. The better your food is digested within the mouth and stomach, the easier it is on your intestines.

Pancreatic enzymes, whether from food or natural supplements, promote health by more efficiently converting food to usable nutrients and energy, which is the sole purpose for eating.

Too much undigested protein escaping from the small intestines into the bloodstream can cause disease. This undigested protein is attacked in the blood as if it were an invader. Circulating immune complexes (CICs) form, making you sick. This is where healthy pancreatic enzymes come into play. They break down the CICs so they can pass through the kidneys for proper excretion. Because of their ability to "clean out" foreign proteins, pancreatic enzymes can also purge infections, viruses, and scar tissue, and aid in the defeat of cancerous tumors.

Pancreatic enzymes expose toxins at the site of cancer cells. Here, the toxins are identified as foreign substances and then destroyed by the body's own natural immune system. When cancerous cells shed toxins, pancreatic enzymes help destroy the residue in the bloodstream, preventing toxic circulation throughout the body. Elimination is critical when healing an illness, particularly cancer.

Pancreatic enzymes also stimulate natural killer cells, T-cells, and anticancer agents. These enzymes actually enter cancer cells in their reproductive phase before they are completely formed and more susceptible to being destroyed. Vitamin A increases this effect because it releases enzymes in the digestive system. The combination of the two types of digestive enzymes has been known to dissolve tumors.

DIGESTION ISN'T JUST IN THE STOMACH

Let me share a story explaining why enzymes are so important.

Bill was a bus driver who experimented over a period of years with various nutrients from the health food store. Taking one vitamin at a time, he'd see how they affected his health. One evening he reported what he thought were unrelated events. Bill had taken some pancreatic enzymes and his nasal allergies cleared up. "Could digestive enzymes be affecting my nasal passages?" he asked.

Yes, they can. Enzymes in the bloodstream can digest foreign protein in the body outside of the digestive tract – even in the nasal passages or any other tissues in the body.

Pollen is approximately 50 percent protein. When it enters the body, this or any other foreign protein will cause toxic reactions if not properly detoxified or digested. Foreign or undigested protein is highly toxic to the body anywhere it makes contact.

There is no reason digestion must be confined to the digestive tract. On the contrary, there is abundant biological proof that proteins can be digested (broken down into their constituent amino acids) anywhere the proteolytic, or protein digesting enzymes, are present under the right conditions of temperature, moisture, etc. Thus, digestive enzymes can effectively digest foreign protein anywhere in the body if these enzymes are present and in contact with these foreign proteins. Therefore, these proteolytic enzymes are an integral and necessary part of the immune system and disease recovery.

So, digestion can take place anywhere in the body where these enzymes are found.

It is well known that these enzymes are produced in the pancreas and enter the small intestines just below the stomach through the common bile duct, where they digest the foreign protein going through the intestinal tract. What is not well known is that a healthy person produces an excess of these enzymes over and above the amount needed for digestion of food protein, and that the excess is picked up by the blood and carried to every cell in the body. These enzymes are found in the blood of all healthy people.

People with cancer typically need more digestive enzymes. This is one of the reasons Drs. Richardson and Krebs identified cancer as a "deficiency disease."

People with allergies tend to develop cancer at a higher rate than people who are relatively free from allergies. Both are caused by toxicity in the body and inadequate elimination of toxins. Statistically, there is never cancer at the juncture of the common bile duct and the small intestine. There is certainly cancer above this point in the mouth, esophagus, and stomach. There is cancer below this point in both the small and large intestines, but there is a curious relationship here. In direct proportion, the further down the intestinal tract from the common bile duct, the greater the incidence of cancer. What enters the intestines through the common bile duct that has such potent anti-cancer effect? The protein digestive enzymes.

<u>So, pancreatic enzymes are able to control even nasal allergies because digestion by enzymes of pollen and other foreign protein can, and do, take place in the nasal passages and other tissues of the body.</u> Dosage recommendations of up to four tablets four times a day are sometimes suggested for severe problems. Enzymes are essentially non-toxic.

Pancreatic enzymes can be found in the blood of the healthy person, but they cannot be found in the blood of the cancer patient. The enzyme producing capacity of the cancer patient is commonly reduced and is overloaded by the food proteins that are depleting the total proteolytic enzyme output; so none remain to be picked up by the blood.

Vegetarians have a much lower incidence of cancer than meat eaters because they are not overloading their digestive capacity. People on a high meat protein diet need more hydrochloric acid-producing capacity in the stomach and a higher output of proteolytic enzymes than do vegetarians.

Statistics show that 50 percent of Americans over 40 do not produce enough acid in the stomach. These same figures are accurate for enzyme production as well.

RAW - THE RIGHT KIND OF FOOD

Raw foods contain enzymes needed for digestion. Ideally, no meal should be eaten that is fully cooked. Animal and human studies have shown that when a fully cooked meal is eaten, the body treats that food as a foreign invader and builds antibodies in the blood against the food. These antibodies are a second component of the body's immune system. When at least 75 percent of the meal is raw, no antibodies appear in the blood. Therefore, at least 75 percent of every meal should be raw.

This percentage of raw food should ideally be increased to one 100 percent for reversal of allergies, cancer, Rheumatoid Arthritis,

Multiple Sclerosis and other diseases that require a toxic load be eliminated. (More on the 75/25 Eating Plan in Chapter Four.)

An old-school nutritional tip: the most nourishing food known to man and animals is liver, but be choosy where you purchase liver. The better health food stores carry predigested raw, desiccated liver tablets made from beef or buffalo that have never been given antibiotics, growth hormones, pesticides or herbicides. The dosage of nine tablets a day, approximately 13.5 grams for cancer patients, rapidly builds the health of the body's liver - the main organ of detoxification and integral part of the body's immune system.

In nature, a predator will eat the liver first from its prey, as the liver houses the most blood and blood nutrients of any body organ. Eating liver restores your liver.

Eating right is vital to health because food provides the fuel human beings need to stay alive. Food converts into raw energy. All food passes through the same set of reactions, whether it is a fast food hamburger or a raw, organic carrot. But enzymes are always needed. Food that is manufactured in a laboratory doesn't provide enzymes, so our bodies have to supply them. When our bodies' supplies of enzymes and nutrients are depleted due to cancer, we must replenish the enzymes somehow; not in fast food lines, not with fat-free, sugar-free food substitutes, not with manmade food replacements, but with whole foods and natural organic supplements. Only with whole foods can human beings maintain the proper supply of the parts that keep the machinery going.

Some good sources of digestive enzymes are:
- Aloe vera
- Honey
- Juice or powdered greens such as wheat grass and barley
- Garlic
- Papaya
- Pineapple

Make sure these foods are raw, cold pressed, and enzyme-active.

VITAMIN C

The most affective form of vitamin C is ascorbic acid NOT sourced from highly processed corn syrup. Ascorbic acid removes toxins from the water stores within your body better than any other form of vitamin C, and ideally, every cell within your body is immersed in water. When the ascorbic acid levels have successfully reached all your cells, the excess vitamin C excretes in your stool, which may make it soft and watery.

Today, there is an ongoing debate on the importance of vitamin C. I support the old school of thought that vitamin C is essential for good health and is needed in larger amounts than the current Recommended Daily Allowance. As previously mentioned, natural vitamin C is best found as ascorbic acid not from a concentrated corn base because some people have a reaction to corn-based vitamin C, creating nausea, intestinal gas, or cramping. This may be due to the high fructose corn base and not the vitamin itself.

Vitamin C is important for:
- Normal growth and development
- Collagen formation in connective tissues and healthy skin
- The healing of wounds and in the recovery from surgery
- Adrenal gland function and hormone production, especially in times of high stress

Pure vitamin C helps in:
- Proper cholesterol metabolism
- Bile production for good digestion
- Alcohol, drug, and smoking detoxification
- Proper iron absorption
- Protecting against pollution and free radicals

A deficiency of vitamin C causes a failure of the cementing substance that holds the cells of the body together. Vitamin C cannot be stored in the body, so it should be provided every day to keep the body in optimum health. Diets low in vitamin C constitute fragile bones. A partial deficiency of vitamin C results in weariness and fatigue accompanied by fleeting pains in the joints and limbs. These pains are often mistaken for arthritis in adults and growing pains in children.

A severe deficiency of vitamin C results in scurvy, a thinning of the blood just under the skin. Years ago when people developed spring fever, referred to today as the first sign of "hay fever" and "allergies," a generous dose of fresh fruits and vegetables, tomatoes, and citrus juices were eaten to relieve the symptoms. Raw vegetables worked well, too.

Unlike most other animals, the human body is unable to produce its own vitamin C. Humans, guinea pigs, apes, and one species of bat found in India are the only animals known to mankind that are unable to produce vitamin C within their own livers. *Now I know why my dog never catches a cold!*

A 150-pound animal produces an average of fifteen grams of vitamin C every day. When the animal is stressed, the liver produces as much vitamin C as needed to meet the demands on its body. Some animals have been known to produce up to 100 grams (100,000 mg.) of vitamin C in one day when put under extreme stress. Yet, humans depend on their diet exclusively for their supply of vitamin C. When under stress, we require more than average daily requirements.

Cooking destroys vitamin C, so it is important to include in your diet two or more servings of a raw vegetable or fruit every day. The more common foods containing vitamin C are:
- Oranges
- Grapefruits
- Tomatoes
- Pineapple

- Raw vegetables
- Green peppers
- Asparagus
- Potatoes
- Turnips
- Bananas
- Strawberries
- Cantaloupe
- Cabbage
- Peas
- Watermelon

The human body is fueled by basic whole foods rich in vitamins and minerals, fibers, enzymes, amino acids, and proteins providing everything human beings need to maintain an energetic healthy life. It's time to get back to the basics of eating to prevent disease.

- For more on vitamin C and cancer, see Chapter 5, "The Significance of vitamin C and Cancer."
- For information on where to find B17 supplements, visit http://www.vitaminb17.de.

CHAPTER 3

The Little Cyanide Cookbook

Contrary to popular belief, cyanide in minute quantities and in the proper form has been proven to be an essential component of normal body chemistry. Instead of a deadly poison, nutritionists "in-the-know" believe cyanide is one of nature's cancer controls. In 1970, June de Spain wrote in The Little Cyanide Cook Book about the foods basic to good nutrition. In her writings, she carefully outlines the foods containing natural cyanide and catalogs the vitamin B17 foods sources found within the major food groups.

According to de Spain, fruits are exceptionally high in B17, some higher than others. Wild varieties are higher in nutrients than crossbred varieties. For example, wild choke cherries, cranberries, and crabapples are much higher in B17 than their hybrid counterparts.

Everyone requires several servings of fruits each day. Ripe fruits contain needed enzymes, minerals from the soil, and vitamin A. Purchase fruits grown in composted and natural soils. And eat their seeds, too! Fruit seeds are rich in protein, polyunsaturated oils, vitamin A, B-Complex, large amounts of vitamin E, AND B17.

The darker the fruit, the more roughage content and pro-vitamin A provided. A dark apricot has a far richer vitamin store than its pale counterpart, and remember, B17 concentrates within the inner seed.

Have you heard of agar-agar? In the 1960's and 1970's, agar-agar was used quite a bit in food processing because it thickens and emulsifies better than any other food. Agar-agar can absorb up to 200 times its volume of water, making a form of jelly.

Agar-agar is popular among vegetarians because it is derived from a very special type of seaweed RICH in nutrients. Agar-agar is a cornucopia of ocean minerals, which nourish the thyroid gland, the pituitary and endocrine systems. Made of sea algae from the Orient, agar-agar is known in some parts of the world as Japanese Kanten.

Agar-agar keeps bowel movements regular by swelling to many times its bulk when it reaches the intestines, increasing peristaltic action and elimination of waste. Daily elimination is critical when detoxing from cancer.

SALADS

Salads are a very important part of the daily diet. Everything but the kitchen sink can be added to a salad. Try a wide variety of fruits and vegetables with every salad serving. Salad vegetables should always be stored in a dry, cold place - never wet. Dry thoroughly before storing, otherwise water withdraws vitamins and minerals from the plant through osmosis. The following is a list of foods that can be included with salads, and some ingredients are rich in vitamin B17*:

watercress*	peas
spinach*	carrots
bamboo sprouts*	tomatoes
alfalfa sprouts*	radishes
lentil sprouts*	whole nuts*
mung bean sprouts*	ground nuts*
garbanzo sprouts*	bell peppers
red cabbage	onions
green cabbage	scallions
romaine lettuce	garlic
red tip lettuce	marinated "leftovers"

chard	chives
dandelion greens	chilies
water chestnuts	asparagus
shallots	cooked brown rice
leeks	marinated garbanzo beans*
orange	coconut
celery	fish
bibb lettuce	chicken
endive	lean roast beef
Chinese cabbage	lemon
broccoli	cauliflower

Salad dressings should be made fresh whenever possible; avoid bottled or packaged with dry herbs. Commercial salad dressings are typically filled with chemical preservatives and chemical flavor enhancers. If you don't have time to make your own dressing or simply want a change, choose dressings with the fewest ingredients possible. The fewer ingredients in anything you buy prepackaged - the more natural the product will be, and the healthier for disease recovery.

VEGETABLES

Vegetables are a very important part of balanced nutrition. Tend a little garden if you can and grow vegetables at home. Use organic fertilizers, no chemical pesticides, and secure a high vitamin and mineral content in the soil.

Having a degree in International Geography, I know only in the United States can so much food be grown by so few farmers. Compared to other countries, the United States is geographically positioned at a perfect latitude to maintain an ample growing season. Therefore, one American farmer alone can feed over 200 people. Two-thirds of Russia and one-half of Europe are located at latitudes above the American-Canadian border, so these countries have a limited growing season. One farmer in Russia feeds less than 20 people.

America has beautiful farmlands yielding a variety of year-round crops, but Americans must be careful not to exploit the soil. Vitamins and minerals found in soils *are* decreasing due to overuse. Plants are cross-bred, "hy-brid", and re-bred to create higher yields, resistance to disease and insect infestation, and quicker growing cycles. The greater the influence modern technology has over natural foods, the further from basic nourishment foods become. If nitrogen, phosphorus, potash and potassium are added to soils, for example, most plants can be forced to grow. When these chemicals premiered inorganically through manufacturing, many farmers stopped rotating their crops in order to replenish the natural nitrogen levels found in the soils. Nutrition is now being sacrificed for higher yields.

Soil is the sole source for all the minerals a plant contains. Climate, humidity, soil conditions, genetics, light, aeration, and soil temperature determine color, size, texture, flavor, disease and insect resistance, vitamin and mineral content, and protein levels of vegetables. The essential minerals present in the soil fundamental to plants are:

- Calcium
- Phosphorus
- Sodium
- Potassium
- Magnesium
- Manganese
- Copper
- Iron
- Zinc
- Iodine
- Chromium
- Cobalt
- Sulfur
- Molybdenum

These are minerals fundamental to human health. The minerals in soils come from the rocks that make up the soil, and all rocks contain essential elements. All living things are comprised of the same elements. Human beings require these elements for normal body function. Bones and teeth are like rocks and rock formations - they all require calcium. Salty human tears are like the salt water in oceans - each made of sodium. Human skin is made of the same minerals as beach sand - both are made of silica. Human beings and nature are connected when it comes to what we each are made of and what each needs to maintain health.

CANDY

June de Spain writes an interesting chapter on candy and, keep in mind, her book was written in the 1970s before the onslaught of pharmaceuticals and the diet craze. Candy seemed more of a particular treat in the 1970s than today but, then as now, candy itself is not necessarily the bad guy. One of the problems with sweets, according to de Spain, is too many sweets discourage an appetite for other foods, so they should be kept to a minimum.

Sugar-free sweets with artificial sugar additives are not the answer, either. Sugar-free does not mean responsibility-free. Too many artificial sweeteners can be as harmful, if not more harmful, than eating too much sugar, especially if battling cancer or another degenrative disease. The amount of unnatural chemicals in many artificial sugar substitutes have toxic by-products.

Simply: keep candy and sweets to a minimum. Use sorghum molasses, rich in vitamin B17, or local honey in place of refined sugar and artificial sweeteners. Provide candy substitutes such as dried fruits high in vitamin B17. They satisfy a sweet tooth and are high in vegetable protein, vitamins, and minerals. Include dried apricots, dates, raisins, apples, cherries, prunes, pears, and peaches. Raw nuts and seeds, popcorn, and soy nuts are good substitutes, too.

A delicious replacement for candy is "fruit leather." Western pioneers made fruit leather. It can be made by pureeing raw, fresh fruit in the blender. Pour into thin sheets onto a cookie sheet lined with waxed paper. Let it dry for about three days in a slightly warm oven. Roll it up in its waxed paper lining and store in a cool, dry place. Freeze it if you like. Fruit leather is not dry or sticky. It doesn't require refrigeration. It satisfies a sweet tooth, and is a chemical-free food rich in vitamin B17. It's a sweet snack that is good for you.

A food tip: when you bake sweets, use whole wheat flour, honey or sorghum cane syrup rich in vitamin B17 and natural extracts. Above all, don't use alkalizers such as baking powder or bicarbonate of soda. These neutralize stomach acids, contain metals, and destroy important B-Complex vitamins.

Avoid hardened and hydrogenized fats such as margarine and Crisco®-type baking fats when preparing sweets and desserts, and forgo artificial colors. Avoid cooking fruits in desserts, too. Cooking kills valuable digestive enzymes. Eat all fruit raw. Raw fruit and natural cheeses make delicious desserts. Add raw nuts and your desserts will be not only tasty, but healthy.

BEVERAGES

In the 1970s, colas (or soft drinks as we call them in the South) were not as widespread as today. Soft drinks were not available in public schools, there were not as many drive-through restaurants from which to purchase a soft drink with every meal, neither was the "big gulp" available for all to buy at the quick mart.

Beverages should ideally be thirst-quenching, refreshing, and nourishing. Instead of colas, especially diet sodas, drink 100 percent fruit juices NOT from concentrate. Pour the juices into a frosty mug or add natural ice cream (ice milk or frozen yogurt) for a sweet treat. Create your own sodas by adding sparkling water or spring water to fruit juices or to milk with ice cream. Puree fruits and add sparkling water with a squeeze of lime.

Limit the number of soft drinks you consume daily. If you must drink a carbonated soda, drink a regular soft drink as opposed to a diet cola. Diet colas are especially harmful when recovering from disease. Natural health food markets offer herbal colas and natural beverages that taste like the old-fashioned colas from the past.

COLAS AND CALCIUM

Soft drink machines have no place in public schools, in my opinion as a mother and a nutritionist. Carbonated beverages offer school-aged children <u>nothing</u> nutritionally. As a geologist, I compare carbonated soft drinks reacting in the human body to water dripping in a cave. Think about this:

Caves form where thick layers of limestone rock containing carbon are found. Water trickles through the soil, turning slightly acid from the carbon dioxide in the air and from decaying plants in the soil. This acidic water dissolves the carbonates (carbon) in the limestone. Over a period of time, the water fills with carbonates and other dissolved minerals it collects along the way. The primary mineral dissolved in cave water is calcite, or calcium. But iron, manganese, and other metals can be found in the water as well. These minerals are responsible for staining caves with beautiful colors. Water dripping from cave roofs form beautiful formations called stalactites and stalagmites. This mineral combination is known as calcium carbonate.

When you open a cola, it fizzes. The "fizz" comes from the tiny bubbles of carbon dioxide trapped inside the sealed container. Carbon dioxide is a byproduct of carbon. Every time you breathe out, you put carbon dioxide into the air. It is one of your body's waste products.

When you drink a carbonated soft drink, you are drinking dissolved carbon, like cave water. Burp the dioxide and the remaining carbon flows through your body like calcium-rich water trickling through a cave. The acidic water from the soft drink dissolves the other minerals in your body it collected along the way, specifically the calcium it assembled from your bones and teeth. Your body disposes of the dissolved minerals by crystallizing the calcium in "your cave" (your body) in the form of bone spurs and arthritis pain. Stalactites and stalagmites of the soul!

In a nutshell, sodas combine with the calcium in your body to form calcium carbonate, just as in a cave. This is not wise, especially for the diet of young children. Many people currently blame the problem with soft drinks on the caffeine or the sugar content. It is important to recognize the primary chain of events created by the soft drink itself as the fundamental concern.

JUICE

So, juice! Buy a juicer and juice ice-cold fresh vegetables and fruits. Vegetable juices are terrific when mixed with fruit juices. Beet juice and strawberry juice go great together. Celery juice blends well with pineapple juice. Carrot juice and coconut milk with a pinch of ground apricot kernels (loaded with B17) are delicious.

For an adult, dark red wines are beneficial to good health. Rich red wines are bursting with essential vitamins and minerals. The darker the wine, the richer its nutrient value, including vitamin B17. Don't overdo, but a glass of good wine can lower stress and blood pressure by feeding the body natural nutrients.

DAIRY

The problem with dairy for most people isn't because it is *dairy*. The problem is more how dairy products are processed, pasteurized, stored, sterilized, preserved, and marketed in modern times, as well as the condition of the animal at the time of milking. A primary source of infectious substances in milk is from infected udders, which spreads infection to the milk at milking, and many of these pathogens are able to survive in significant numbers.

The pasteurization of milk has been under increasing scrutiny due to the discovery of pathogens remaining after pasteurization that are both widespread and heat resistant. In recent years, this fact has renewed consumer interest in raw milk products. (see below for more on pasteurization)

So, let's back up and focus on dairy for what it is supposed to be. Raw dairy that has not been pasteurized contains immunoglobulins and the digestive enzymes lipase and phosphatase, which are inactivated by heat. Raw milk also contains vitamin B6 of which up to 20 percent may be lost during pasteurization and heat treatments. Raw milk also contains beneficial bacteria which aid digestion and boost immunity.

The three major milk cultures are:
- Buttermilk
- Kefir
- Yogurt

In the "olden days", milk cultures were part of the daily diet - and well they should be. Any or all of these dairy foods (if you can find them in modern markets) can be used to make your own milk cultures. They all have the same nutritional advantages of raw milk.

THICK MILK

THICK MILK (also known as claubber, soured, and whole milk): Add 1/4 cup buttermilk to 2 cups certified (organic) milk. Cover the container and set it aside for 24 hours to allow it to form a tangy custard with both curds and whey. The whey is naturally high in calcium. Keep this in mind if you drink a lot of soft drinks. You can use some of the "thick milk" to start a new batch, too. Mold may form, but it is harmless. Simply scrape off the mold, and use it to make cheese. What a nutrient rush, especially if you have calcium deficiencies!

KEFIR

KEFIR: Add 1/4 cup unflavored kefir to 2 cups certified milk. Cover the container and set it aside for 48 hours. The resulting custard is mildly sour, but what a yogurt drink! Put the kefir culture in the blender with fruit and fruit juices and create a tasty, nutritious, natural drink.

YOGURT

YOGURT: Take 1/4 cup unflavored, commercial yogurt and add 2 cups certified milk. Cover and set for 72 hours. The resulting custard is very sour, but it's nutritionally rich primarily because pathogenic bacteria do not live in lactic acid. If you have a gastrointestinal problem, the more sour the yogurt, the more beneficial to you. Serve with fruit, honey, sorghum, or maple syrup, and make the healthiest yogurt in the world. Mix with a fruit drink and make slushy ice cream or a smoothie.

Avoid powdered milks. They are cooked and are high in artificial vitamin D and strontium. Excessive strontium alters proper calcium absorption. A little bit of dried milk goes a long way, but a cup or more a day can be toxic. Highly concentrated powdered milks are found in some protein powders and pills. Combined with a vigorous workout regimen, concentrated doses of powdered milk products can be toxic for many weight lifters and athletes.

Why was dairy once a good thing, but now it's a not-so-good thing? What has changed dairy?

PASTEURIZATION

Pasteurization, for one thing. I've always wanted to know why is it unlawful to sell unpasteurized milk in the United States today. Shouldn't it be the consumer's choice?

Pasteurization is the process by which milk and other fluid foods are sterilized. The procedure is called "pasteurization" after Louis Pasteur, a 19th century scientist. Pasteur was paid to investigate problems French wine growers were having with fermentation. During his research, he discovered that heating milk to a temperature slightly below boiling point would effectively stop fermentation and prevent milk from spoiling. This heating also destroyed diseased organisms that would have been passed on to consumers. As a result of his studies on pasteurization, Pasteur in turn identified the tuberculosis bacillus known as "Tuberculosis," the most prominent lung infection affecting mankind.

Today, pasteurization has transformed dairy past the point that Louis Pasteur had intended. Pasteurization has completely annihilated all nutritive value in dairy products.

Pasteurization is normally achieved by heating milk for about 40 minutes at a temperature around 140-1600°F (60-700°C). However, this heating destroys the vitamin C in milk, chemically alters milk sugar or lactose, and metabolizes the fat and carbohydrate stores within milk protein. These components of raw unpasteurized milk are needed in their natural form to aid in chemical reactions within the body because the body requires raw energy from the milk to support bones and teeth. As a result of heating, the vitamins and minerals in the milk begin to metabolize or break down before the body receives them. In other words, the milk has already been broken down before the body is able to use it. We are, therefore, drinking "moot" milk. It does the body *little* good.

Combine "moot milk" with "cavernous sodas", and you are drinking non-productive beverages with failing nutritional value, creating malnutrition in modern humans. It would be worthwhile to reestablish the minimal degree to which milk is pasteurized.

Dr. Burkitt's work in Africa (see Chapter 5, BURKITT'S CANCER DISCOVERY) revealed the same conclusion about cancer drugs; Americans have taken the technology beyond a steady state. We discovered a good thing but took it way beyond a natural balance. Dairy products are subjected to an overkill of pasteurization.

MEATS

Meats are an important part of an animal's diet, but are not fundamental if all the essential amino acids are supplied by other sources. Meats are considered a complete protein food because they contain the "basic eight" essential amino acids. Flesh and organs from freshly-killed animals incorporate all amino acids and essential vitamins and minerals needed for healthy survival.

Any animal killed in the wild first forfeits its liver and other organs over muscle because of the abundant nutritional content. An animal's blood is rich in B17, iron, iodine, zinc, and other minerals. Wild animals do not worry about fat content because fat contains high levels of vitamin A. Primitive man ate this way, and wild animals still do. So should modern man.

Today, meat is aged and cured for an average of 10 to 15 days. This produces a more tender product, but one absent of original vitamins and minerals. Wild animals will pass over processed meats when given the choice between processed or natural.

When possible, eat organic or wild meats. Domesticated meats may contain hard fats and insecticide residues. Pork may embody dyes, nitrates, nitrites and carcinogenic preservatives, large quantities of salt, and an abundance of unknown chemicals. Cook lean and tender meats as little as possible to retain the nutrients. If a cut of meat is tough, gently cook over low heat for a longer period of time.

If possible, buy free-range chickens. Free-range chickens do not spend their existence caged, but are provided proper space to move around. Fed natural grains with fewer antibiotics, hormones, and antioxidants, free-range chickens provide higher quality meat with a lesser amount of hard fat and a greater amount of natural nutrients. Chickens should be cooked over low heat and never overcooked. Any stock or gravy can be used for soups and sauces. Boil the bones several hours with wine or apple cider vinegar for a soup base rich in vitamins and digestive aids.

Note: All animal protein, including dairy products, should be excluded during cancer recovery. After health has been restored to the body, organic meats and dairy can be slowly reintroduced.

The Little Cyanide Cookbook can be ordered through American Media, P.O. Box 4646, Westlake, CA, 91359.

CHAPTER 4

Morale Food

Generally when I'm researching a book, I seek out the oldest, most prized books I can find; books replete with wisdom from the ages. Flipping the pages of a nutrition cookbook I had stumbled upon, I abruptly stopped reading when the words *"Morale Food"* caught my eye.

"Morale Food"? Foods that promote a feeling of general wellbeing and increased vigor were called "morale foods" 60 years ago. "Naturally, vitamins are found in foods in minute amounts," I read, "but they influence vital body processes in enormous ways. Vitamin rich foods can promote a positive mental attitude."

Now here's a simple fact, but one that isn't emphasized enough these days! Human bodies operate the same today as 10,000 years ago, but our foods and diseases aren't the same as even 20 years ago. Here is a connection to the cause of many diseases and depression.

At least nine vitamins are crucial to human nutrition, but if your diet provides merely vitamins A, B, (especially B1), C, and G (riboflavin), chances are the other vitamins will be found in adequate amounts in the same food sources. Vitamin D, however, does not occur in large enough quantities in foods to be significant, and it is recommended that a special source such as fish liver oil, natural supplements, and sunshine be provided.

Good nutrition is simple. Basic nutrition doesn't need to be as complicated as food manufacturers and crafty advertisers make it out to be. Fat-free this and sugar-free, low-carb this and no-carb that. How far from the common sense of eating we human animals have wandered; especially modern-day children. The old nutrition books from years ago are great to read because they kept nutrition simple.

Diseases have plagued mankind for centuries. In the 1940s, diseases were directly traced to the lack of one or more vitamins in the diet; not to the multitude of artificial, manmade chemicals polluting our foods and our bodies. *All vitamins* contribute to health and general wellbeing. Each vitamin functions in a highly specialized way to secure human health, a natural miracle. The complications of modern nourishment have set aside the simple basics of yesteryear. Food has become more complicated, and disease has become equally as complicated.

FOOD FOR ENERGY

Food for energy! Food is primarily needed to provide energy for daily activities. The human body is like a machine. A machine burns gasoline or coal for fuel; the human body burns food for fuel. It's as simple as that. A machine converts its fuel into other forms of energy; the human body converts its food into body energy.

The unit used for measuring the amount of energy in food is called the CALORIE. All foods furnish calories, but in different amounts. Two heads of lettuce, one egg, three lumps of sugar, and one teaspoon of butter all furnish 75 calories, but they are entirely different from one another.

The three chief sources of energy are:
- Fats
- Carbohydrates
- Proteins

Foods high in fat, such as butter, cream, and salad dressings, contain more calories per unit of weight than foods largely composed of carbohydrates like sugar, breads, cereals, or proteins found in eggs, cheese, and meat. Lettuce is low in calories, but is made mostly of cellulose, a substance the body typically does not use. Lettuce does move wastes out of the colon, however, as it passes through the body. Tomato juice is low in calories because it is mostly water.

PROTEIN

Protein is one of the three sources of energy required for body-building material. The word protein comes from the Greek word "to come first." Without protein, neither life nor growth is possible. Children need more protein in proportion to their weight than adults because they are growing rapidly. Adults need protein for the maintenance of body tissues. Only in cases of pregnancy, lactation, and in the recovery from wasting diseases do adults need protein for growth.

There are many kinds of proteins, some superior to others in nutritive value. Organic milk, cheese, eggs, meat and fish contain the best quality protein provided by nature.

MINERALS

Minerals are needed for growth. At least 19 different minerals have been found in the human body in varying amounts. However, only a few are given special attention anymore.

Calcium and phosphorus are needed in large amounts because they are necessary for strong bones and teeth. Calcium also plays a part in the regulation of the nervous system and muscular response. It helps maintain the rhythmic beat of the heart and is essential for normal blood clotting. Iron is needed in small amounts but is a very important part of every living cell as well as in the hemoglobin of the blood.

The other essential minerals needed for proper body function are furnished in the foods that supply calcium, iron and protein. *Another reason to eat whole foods, preferably raw!*

CALCIUM

Some of the best sources for calcium are:
- Carrots
- Oranges
- Kale
- Beans
- Broccoli
- Clams
- Milk and milk products (cheese included) are reliable sources of calcium

In the 1940s, it was recommended that every child consume a quart of "pure" milk each day. (See Chapter 3) An adult required at least a pint to adequately provide the calcium needed to sustain proper health. Why is this so different today – what's changed? Our bodies or our foods?

During pregnancy, the demands for calcium are obviously higher since a baby's development in addition to the mother's requirements must be provided. Every expectant mother should drink at least a quart of "pure" milk a day. If she doesn't receive the proper calcium from food, the growing fetus will be supplied at the expense of her bones and teeth. At the turn of the 20th century, the expression, *"A tooth for every child"* was true. Little has changed over time.

IRON

Iron is essential in the formation of hemoglobin and gives the blood its red color. It is responsible for transporting oxygen to the cells. Foods that provide iron are:
- Egg yolks
- Liver
- Kidney
- Heart and lean meats
- Oysters
- Shrimp
- Clams
- Green leafy vegetables
- Whole grain cereals
- Potatoes
- Molasses
- Apricots
- Prunes

Insufficient iron in the diet results in listliness, pallor, and poor appetite. The normal requirement for iron is really small, but most foods today contain such tiny amounts of iron, it is difficult to get enough natural iron. Make an effort to eat iron-rich foods every day, especially growing children and pregnant and lactating women.

IODINE

Iodine is a special mineral that is also overlooked in modern diets. I discovered this when I cured my thyroid disease. Iodine aids the thyroid gland and assists in sugar metabolism. If you have a thyroid problem, diabetes, or hypoglycemia, make sure to get enough iodine in your diet. Foods which provide iodine are:
- Iodized salt, preferably sea salt
- Fish liver oils
- Sea and shellfish (fresh or canned)

- Fruits and vegetables grown in coastal soils

Iodine is a problem in "the goiter belts", regions shut off from the spray of the sea. These are regions located by mountain ranges or inland locations. A special effort must be made in these regions to supply sufficient iodine in the diet.

WATER

Water is important in keeping the body strong. Two-thirds of the adult human body is water - salt water. Humans drink fresh water, but their bodies are 75 percent saline. Simply taste a tear or a bead of sweat for its salt content. This is one reason why humans need to drink ample amounts of fresh water every day. It keeps the body's salt concentrations low, easing stress on the kidneys and preventing dehydration. Plus, the average adult eliminates approximately eight cups of water a day by sweating, urinating, crying, and creating saliva. It is essential to replace what is lost.

Instead of drinking sodas throughout day, get into the habit of walking around with a bottle of water - all day long. You'll have more energy, feel better, feel full, and flush out toxins with proper urination.

All of our body's cells float in water. As a matter of fact, they reproduce in a watery base. If there is insufficient water available in your body, the cells have difficulty duplicating. This can cause an assortment of problems. Water provides the liquid medium for the blood, for the digestive juices, and the elimination of waste. Water is critical for the regulation of body temperature, too. Drink water more than any other liquid, especially after meals to aid in digestion.

Never drink liquids while eating. Your mouth contains digestive juices necessary to begin the digestive process, and washing down your food with liquids washes away the digestive enzymes in the saliva. Drink *after* you have completely swallowed your food or after the meal.

Just as nutritious foods can promote a feeling of general wellbeing and increased vigor, a partial deficiency of vitamins can create a vague, overall feeling of being rundown, and generally results in a lowered resistance to infection, increased nervousness, fatigue, and a poor appetite. A diet of nutritionally-void foods such as fat-free, sugar-free, bleached, processed foods can create depression and can increase feelings of stress.

Eating shouldn't be complicated. Why don't we go back to the simplicity of eating, like during our grandparents' days? Maybe then we could begin enjoying food again, feeling better, having more energy, and acting less stressed out.

B Vitamins

Foods containing the B vitamins, especially vitamin B1, are considered potent morale foods because they promote a feeling of general wellbeing and increased vigor.

Vitamin B1 is also called thiamine. A severe deficiency of thiamine is associated with diseases of the nervous system and poor digestion, resulting in overall poor health. Many oriental countries suffer with these types of diseases because they eat predominantly polished rice (when the hulls are removed), which is devoid of vitamin B1.

Vitamin B1:
- Maintains a normal appetite
- Promotes good digestion and the absorption of nutrients
- Combats constipation
- Plays an important role in burning carbohydrate foods in the body
- Is essential for normal reproduction and lactation

Vitamin B1 is found in the outer coats and embryos of grains. Polishing rice and the manufactured processing of breads and cereals removes this vitamin. In the United States, the manufacturers of white flour and refined cereals add vitamin B1 back into their processed products, but this isn't the same as eating the vitamin in its natural, original state. I've always wondered where the "enriched vitamins" come from anyway.

Do the manufacturing companies salvage the natural vitamins from their original extraction and insert them back into the processed food products? Do they buy the vitamins from a health food store and dump them into their vats in bulk? Are the "vitamins" merely chemical reproductions of natural vitamins?

Foods that provide natural vitamin B1 include:
- Lean meats
- Liver
- Kidney
- Port
- Yeast
- Whole-grain cereals and flour
- Wheat germ
- Legumes
- Beans
- Peanuts
- Egg yolk
- Milk
- Oranges
- Pineapple
- Grapefruit
- Tomatoes
- Peas
- Potatoes
- Green leafy vegetables

Vitamin B2 is known as riboflavin and helps the body metabolize carbohydrates, fats, and proteins. It is fundamental for red blood cell formation, antibody production, and cell respiration. B2 facilitates the utilization of oxygen for the tissues of the skin, mucous membranes, nails, and hair. This vitamin is needed to properly metabolize niacin. B2 is important in the prevention and treatment of cataracts, and is especially important during pregnancy to help promote healthy fetal growth.

Individuals who take antibiotics or oral contraceptives, drink alcohol daily, or exercise heavily have increased needs for vitamin B2. The best sources are:
- Almonds
- Broccoli
- Cheese
- Green leafy vegetables
- Egg yolks
- Fish
- Legumes
- Milk
- Organ meats
- Poultry
- Soy
- Spinach
- Whole grains
- Yogurt

Vitamin B3, commonly known as niacin, is proven to regulate blood sugar levels, is critical for the synthesis of sex hormones, and detoxifies the body of most manmade drugs and chemicals. It is necessary for healthy mental function, and is necessary for red blood cell formation and blood circulation. B3 lowers cholesterol and is a vasodilator. It assists in the maintenance of skin, nerve, and blood vessels.

Niacin is not found in corn, and people on a corn-based diet are usually deficient in B3. In 1942, niacin was added to enriched flour and other commercially-made products.

B3 is involved in the normal secretion of bile and stomach fluids and is needed for the production of hydrochloric acid, critical for proper food assimilation and digestion. Like the other B vitamins, B3 helps the body metabolize carbohydrates, fats, and protein.

Individuals who are highly toxic or drink alcohol daily have an increased need for vitamin B3. Because they do not metabolize the vitamin efficiently, elderly people and individuals with hyperthyroidism also need higher doses of niacin.

Niacin is found in:
- Brewer's yeast
- Broccoli
- Carrots
- Cheese
- Dandelion greens
- Dates
- Eggs
- Fish
- Milk
- Nuts
- Pork
- Potatoes
- Tomatoes
- Wheat germ

Vitamin B5, also known as Pantothenic Acid, is essential for growth, reproduction, and normal physiological functions, including energy metabolism of carbohydrates, proteins and lipids, the synthesis of lipids, neurotransmitters, steroid hormones, and hemoglobin. It assists in making bile, building red blood cells, and is necessary for the normal functioning of the gastrointestinal tract. B5 has been found helpful in treating depression.

Most plant and animal foods contain B5, and is a very abundant vitamin in whole foods. Natural sources of B5 include:
- Avocado

- Brewer's yeast
- Eggs
- Beans
- Brown rice
- Corn
- Lentils
- Mushrooms
- Nuts
- Organ meats
- Peas
- Pork
- Saltwater fish
- Soybeans
- Sweet potatoes
- Wheat germ

Vitamin B6, pyridoxine, is involved in more bodily functions than almost any other nutrient. This nutrient helps metabolize carbohydrates, fats, and proteins, and supports the immune system, nervous system, and mental functions. B6 is vital for nerve impulse transmission within the brain and is necessary for antibody production.

Pyridoxine maintains the body's sodium-potassium balance, aids in the formation of red blood cells, and helps synthesize RNA and DNA. It protects the heart by inhibiting the formation of homocysteine, a toxic chemical that attacks the heart muscle and contributes to cholesterol deposits around the heart.

B6 is found in:
- Avocados
- Bananas
- Beans
- Blackstrap molasses
- Brown rice
- Carrots
- Corn

- Fish
- Legumes
- Nuts
- Poultry
- Soybeans
- Sunflower seeds
- Tempeh
- Walnuts
- Wheat germ

Vitamin B7 is commonly known as biotin. Best known as a moisturizing agent in shampoos, conditioners, and skin creams, biotin is essential to numerous body processes. As with the other B vitamins, biotin allows the body to metabolize carbohydrates, fats, and proteins, aids in cell growth, is necessary for fatty acid production, and promotes normal function of the sweat glands, nerve tissue, bone marrow, and helps relieve muscle pain.

Most foods contain biotin, which is found in highest concentration in:
- Beef
- Brewer's yeast
- Broccoli
- Egg yolks
- Kidneys
- Milk
- Nuts
- Poultry
- Saltwater fish
- Soybeans
- Sunflower seeds
- Sweet potatoes
- Whole grains

Vitamin B9, folic acid, is necessary in the development of healthy fetuses, preventing low birth weights and premature birth. It is also needed for healthy nervous system functioning, assists in the formation of red blood cells, the metabolism of protein, and the synthesis of DNA and RNA. It is important for cell division and replication. It helps manufacture white blood cells and is necessary for healthy immune system function.

Foods that contain vitamin B9 are:
- Apricots
- Asparagus
- Avocados
- Barley
- Brussels sprouts
- Dried beans
- Brewer's yeast
- Brown rice
- Cantaloupe
- Celery
- Eggs
- Fish
- Mushrooms
- Nuts
- Oranges
- Peas
- Root vegetables
- Seeds
- Tempeh
- Wheat bran
- Wheat germ

Vitamin B12, also known as cobalamin, is best known for its role in preventing anemia. It works with folic acid to help form and regulate red blood cells, absorb and utilize iron. It aids in cellular longevity and in maintaining fertility. Along with the other B vitamins, it helps metabolize carbohydrates, fats, and proteins, and is essential in producing myelin, a fatty substance that forms a protective sheath around the nerves. Vitamin B12 is linked to the production of a neurotransmitter that assists memory and learning.

Unlike the other B vitamins, B12 takes several hours to be absorbed by the digestive tract. While excess vitamin B12 is excreted in the urine, a small "backup" supply is stored for three to five years in the liver.

People taking anticoagulant drugs, antigout medication, or potassium supplements, vegans, the elderly, and people with AIDS have an increased need for vitamin B12.

Vitamin B15, known as Pangamic Acid, is a fairly controversial vitamin. The FDA has been monitoring the wide range of medical conditions treated with B15 in other countries. Pangamic Acid is not readily available in the USA, as the FDA has taken Pangamic Acid products off the market.

Russia has been the most progressive country concerning B15, believing it is a very important nutrient with physiological actions that can treat a multitude of symptoms and diseases. Russian scientists have shown that Pangamic Acid supplementation can reduce the buildup of lactic acid in athletes and thereby lessen muscle fatigue and increase endurance. It is used regularly in Russia for many health problems, including:

- Alcoholism
- Drug addiction
- Aging and senility
- Minimal brain damage in children
- Autism
- Schizophrenia
- Heart disease
- High blood pressure; diabetes
- Skin diseases
- Liver disease
- Chemical poisonings

Dimethyl glycine (DMG) has been used in the United States as a substitute for B15 as it is believed to increase Pangamic Acid production in the body. Dimethyl glycine combines with gluconic acid to form Pangamic Acid. It is thought that the DMG is the active component of Pangamic Acid.

Pangamic Acid is found in:
- Whole grains such as brown rice
- Brewer's yeast
- Pumpkin and sunflower seeds
- Apricot kernels
- Beef blood

B15 helps in the formation of certain amino acids such as methionine. It plays a role in the oxidation of glucose in cell respiration. Like vitamin E, it acts as an antioxidant helping to lengthen cell life through its protection from oxidation. Pangamic Acid mildly stimulates the endocrine and nervous systems, and by enhancing liver function, it helps in the detoxification process.

B15 has been shown to lower blood cholesterol, improve circulation and general oxygenation of cells and tissues, and is helpful for arteriosclerosis and hypertension, America's most common diseases.

In Europe, vitamin B15 has been used to treat premature aging, because of both its circulatory stimulus and its antioxidant effects. It is a helpful protectant from pollutants, especially carbon monoxide. Pangamic Acid (and possibly DMG) offers support for anyone living in a large polluted city or with a high stress level.

As previously mentioned, Pangamic Acid is used in Russia to treat alcohol dependency, and is believed to reduce alcohol cravings. It has been reported to diminish hangovers. B15 has also been used to treat fatigue, as well as asthma and rheumatism, and it may even have some anti-allergen properties. Some child psychiatrists have reported good results using Pangamic Acid with emotionally disturbed children; it may help by stimulating speaking ability and other mental functions. B15 may also be implemented for autism, but more specific research is needed.

It is currently illegal to distribute B15 in the United States, though it was used as a supplement for some time through the 1970s. The most common form of Pangamic Acid is calcium pangamate, but it appears dimethyl glycine (DMG), which may actually be the active component that has been hailed in Russia. Pangamic Acid, or DMG, is often taken with vitamin E and vitamin A. A common amount of DMG is 50–100 mg. taken twice daily, usually with breakfast and dinner. This level of intake may improve general energy levels, support the immune system, and is also thought to reduce cravings for alcohol and thus may be very helpful in moderating chronic alcohol problems.

Vitamin B17 has also been completely eliminated from the complex B-vitamin supplements in the United States, but can be found in nature with foods containing the other B vitamins. According to research provided by nutritionists and medical scientists from decades past, vitamin B17 is a natural cyanide-containing compound that gives up its cyanide content only in the presence of a particular enzyme group called "beta glucosidase" or "glucuronidase." Miraculously, this enzyme group is found almost exclusively in cancer tissue. If found elsewhere, B17 is always accompanied by greater quantities of another enzyme, rhodanese, which has the ability to disable the cyanide and convert it into a completely harmless substance. Cancer tissues do not include rhodanese. Therefore, cancer cells are faced with a double threat; the presence of one enzyme exposing them to cyanide, while the absence of another enzyme found in all other normal cells results in the cancer's failure to detoxify itself. Like all other animals in nature that ingest B17 foods, the cyanide destroys diseased cells. The cancer cells that are unable to withstand the cyanide are destroyed. The non-cancerous cells are not threatened by the cyanide and remain unharmed.

Vitamin B17 is found naturally in many foods. If you eat foods containing vitamin B17, your body will know what to do next. All other animals in nature instinctively seek these nutrients. Consider it nature's cancer prevention. If only modern medicine would allow it to be so.

The following is a list of foods rich in vitamin B17 (also see Chapter 2):

- Watercress
- Spinach
- Bamboo sprouts
- Alfalfa sprouts
- Lentil sprouts
- Whole nuts
- Mung bean sprouts
- Ground nuts
- Garbanzo sprouts
- Apple seeds
- Apricot seeds

So, in a nutshell (no pun intended), you can understand why this vitamin B-Complex is important to restore, replace, and repair damage from toxins.

VITAMIN A

Vitamin A is essential for growth and maintenance of good health at all ages. It helps build the body's resistance to infections, especially in the nose, throat, lungs, eyes, and ears. Vitamin A helps prevent night blindness. It keeps the skin smooth and healthy and maintains tooth enamel. Vitamin A is essential for normal reproduction.

Vitamin A is found in:

- Green leafy vegetables, especially thin green leaves like spinach
- Watercress

- Kale
- The outer dark leaves and inner pale leaves of lettuce
- Cabbage
- Yellow vegetables
- Carrots
- Tomatoes
- Apricots
- Yellow peaches
- Whole, pure milk
- Cream
- Butter
- Egg yolks
- Liver and kidney
- Fish-liver oils

VITAMIN G

Vitamin G, also known as riboflavin or B2, promotes growth, general good health, tones the digestive tract, and postpones senility. A deficiency of vitamin G causes lesions at the corner of the mouth, which clear up when riboflavin is added to the diet. Vitamin G is found in:

- Milk
- Green leafy vegetables
- Egg yolks
- Lean meats
- Kidney and liver
- Wheat germ
- Whole wheat cereals
- Yeast

Vitamin G (B2) is also required for red blood cell formation and respiration, antibody production, and for regulating human growth, and reproduction. It is essential for healthy skin, nails, hair growth and general good health, including regulating thyroid activity.

Natural minerals and vitamins can be lost as a result of careless handling during bulk storage, during the manufacturing and packaging of bulk food products, and through cooking before foods even reach the table. Vitamins B1 and C are destroyed by heat, oxidation, and light, and they both readily dissolve in water. Heat affects vitamin B1 less than it affects vitamin C.

Foods containing these vitamins are exposed to room temperatures and the longer the cooking period, the greater the destruction. Boiling water often dissolves the minerals and some vitamins in foods. Steaming is best. Therefore, foods should be cooked as quickly as possible. Ordinary cooking temperatures do not effect vitamins A and G.

Note: Cooking destroys vitamin C, so it is important to include two or more servings of raw vegetables and fruits every day. Oranges, grapefruits, tomatoes, pineapple (fresh or canned), raw vegetables, green peppers, asparagus, potatoes, turnips, bananas, strawberries, cantaloupe, cabbage, peas, and watermelon are some of the more common foods containing vitamin C.

COOKING RECOMMENDATIONS

- Do not place fruits, vegetables, meats and fresh foods immediately into the refrigerator after you buy them. First, wash fruits and vegetables and place them in a covered pan or hydrator. If a dark place is available, many vegetables and fruits, potatoes and apples will keep well, especially if purchased in large quantities.

- If possible, prepare fruit juices and pare, slice, chop, grate or juice raw fruits and vegetables just before they are used. If it is necessary to prepare them in advance, cover closely and store in the refrigerator until serving time. The loss of vitamin C will be minimal unless the food is kept too long.

- Do not let prepared fruits, vegetables, or fruit juices stand uncovered at room temperature for any period of time. The vitamins go right out.

- Cook foods in a tightly covered container. Resist stirring air into the food during cooking. If cooked food is to be sieved, cool it first.

- Cook foods using the shortest cooking times. Unnecessarily long cooking not only diminishes nutrients but results in inferior flavor, texture, and appearance.

- Do not use soda in vegetable cooking under any circumstances!

- Use the liquids in which foods are cooked or canned. Use them in soups, sauces and gravies. In the case of fruits, use the liquids in desserts and beverages. When a dried fruit or vegetable is soaked before cooking, cook it in the water in which it was soaked.

- Cook vegetables in the least amount of water possible.

- Follow the package's directions when using quick-frozen foods. Do not thaw food before cooking unless directed, and only then, thaw it in the refrigerator.

- Do not let thawed foods stand at room temperature any longer than necessary.

We all should remember to eat like the caveman did. Caveman diets were fresh and raw. Every meal should be 75 percent fresh and raw. Consider your food plate like a pie. Three-quarters (3/4) of the pie should be fresh, raw, or steamed at every meal to properly provide the active enzymes, natural vitamins, minerals, fiber, and protein the human body requires for daily fuel.

For more information on the 75/25 pH Balance Eating Plan, visit:
http://www.janethull.com/ph-balance-testing/

EGGS

An egg is not bad! Free-range, organic eggs are outstanding in their nutritional benefits. The yolk of an egg is the richest source of:
- All the natural essential amino acids
- Sulfur-containing amino acids, rarely found in most foods
- Vitamins A and E
- Biotin
- Choline
- Inositol
- Enzymes
- Protein

All these nutrients are necessary to sustain life.

The egg white contains a good amount of riboflavin and the complete protein albumin, but does little good if not eaten <u>with</u> the yolk.

Raw eggs offer the highest benefits because heat alters their vitamin structure. Heat alters the chemical structure of all matter. In nature, predators love to steal raw eggs from nests. Nature knows how nutritious eggs are. Very rarely will you see an animal steal another's egg without eating it on the spot, and the nutritive value of one egg can sustain an animal for one week if no other food is found.

Don't overcook your eggs. Hard-boiling eggs destroys the lecithin and other cholesterol-protecting substances naturally placed within the egg. Eating eggs softly cooked, if not raw, is a good thing.

An egg yolk grows into new life if allowed to mature. Forming under the warmth of its mother, an egg develops into a bird or reptile, into a human being, into all living animals. Within the yolk are the ingredi-

ents to create *life*. If the yolk is eaten before it forms, the same ingredients that create new life become the nutrients to sustain life. Nature's
liquid yellow vitamin pack!

Industrialized societies have created an egg scare. All the promo-
tion about egg yolks being filled with fat and dangerous cholesterol
is taken out of context by marketers, in my opinion. Before blaming
the egg, think about how the egg is cooked, what other foods you eat
with the egg like greasy meats and fats, Equal® in your coffee, or fake
cheeses half-melted on a bleached white floured biscuit concocted
with fake fats and oils. And, how many eggs do you eat in one meal?
Consider the other factors to this erroneous equation before you
blame the all-natural egg.

FOOD CHEMICALS

Are you eating an assortment of laboratory chemicals every day?
Chemicals are abundant in the average American diet. Chemical food
additives were first invented with the purpose of keeping food safe
and bacteria free. But, technology has taken chemicals way beyond
health and safety. Today, the majority of Western food is saturated
with an onslaught of unnecessary chemicals. Some foods aren't even
real food, simply manmade, petroleum based, fabricated, fake inven-
tions created to replace nature. And chemicals certainly shouldn't be
eaten! There are chemicals to change food color, to enhance flavor, to
make food taste even sweeter. This is unnecessary, it's dangerous, and
it is unwise. And, the overabundance of manufactured food chemicals
can lead to cancer, or at the least, suppress the body's immune system.

CANCER FROM FOODS

<u>Colon cancer</u>: This type of cancer is at its highest level in the United States today because the modern-day "diet of convenience" has promoted the highest fat, lowest fiber, fried food and processed diet in the world.

- The lowest colon cancer rates are found in Japan because the Japanese have diets low in processed fat.
- Mormons also have a low colon cancer rate because they eat a natural food diet, especially a diet high in natural fiber.
- Seventh-Day Adventists have a low colon cancer rate, too, because they eat very low to no fatty fried foods and also have high fiber diets.

<u>Stomach cancer</u>:

- Poses the highest risk in Japan and South America because a high degree of salted and pickled foods is consumed in these two countries. They also add nitrates to their soils and water, and have an average low intake of vitamins C and E.
- Is the lowest in the United States because Americans have fresh fruits, salads, and vitamins C and E available year round.

Beware: fat substitutes absorb the fat-soluble vitamins A, D, E, and K. This is bad news for the body's immune system, cardiovascular system, and digestive system, and particularly the liver. Each of these body systems depends on the above vitamins to keep them healthy. Essential fats should be natural because the body can expel them easily with a good B vitamin and vigorous exercise. The liver and gall bladder cannot assimilate unnatural <u>chemicals</u>, processed fats, anyway. Human bodies haven't evolved that ability.

<u>Breast cancer</u>:

- The highest rate in the United States and Western Europe due to the "Westernized" high-fat, chemical-fat diet.
- The lowest rate in Japan as a result of their low-fat diet.

Prostate cancer:
- The highest rate in the United States and Scandinavia because of high fat contents.
- The lowest rate in Japan due to low fat consumption.

Esophagus cancer:
- The highest rate in France.
- The highest rate within the lower socioeconomic groups in the United States.
- France and the United States have high risk factors of alcohol and tobacco use.
- The highest rate within Eastern Iran and Central China.
- Iran and China have very low levels of vitamins C and A available, and the use of opium possibly causes esophagus cancer.

So, foods _do_ make a difference. My grandmother used to say, *"You don't live to eat; you eat to live."* Grandmommy lived to be 102 years old and gracefully passed away in her home of 100+ years.

CHAPTER 5

Nutrition Case Histories: Cancers, Tumors, Cysts

CANCER OF THE JAWBONE
METASTASIZED TO THE BRAIN AND LUNGS

On the evening of August 18, 1984, arrangements were made for the Head of the Ugandan Armed Forces, James Odongo, to begin an anti-cancer treatment developed in the 1970s by American medical doctor John Richardson. Odongo's wife, The Ugandan Deputy Minister of Health, anxiously observed at his bedside.

Odongo was dying of jaw cancer. His case was not unusual. Cancers show marked regional variations in most African countries, and cancer of the jaw is common in Uganda. The source is unknown. Jaw cancer is prevalent in Ugandan children.

Disease patterns vary enormously across Africa. Killer diseases are present everywhere. In underprivileged areas, illnesses are often associated with poverty and inadequate nutrition. In more privileged regions, nutritional deficiencies and infectious diseases sourced to poor waste disposal and contaminated water supplies are less common. Nonetheless, these regions suffer with degenerative diseases such as strokes and cancer.

General Odongo's cancer first developed at the site of an abscessed tooth. In 1981, West German physicians removed his right jawbone and told him they removed all the cancer. Odongo was 39 years old at the time.

The cancer came back. It spread to his brain, leaving him terminally ill. The best physicians in West Germany, England, and Italy treated him with radiation and chemotherapy. All gave up on him. His metastasis continued to progress. By January 1984, he could not talk. He was paralyzed on his left side. As a last resort, he was brought to the United States in July that same year.

Odongo's personal physician was Head of the Cancer Institute in Uganda. He accompanied General Odongo to a renowned university hospital in Tulsa, Oklahoma. American doctors operated and removed part of the tumor, now the size of a turkey egg. After the operation, Odongo's head swelled over twice its normal size. The cancer spread to both his lungs. He lost his appetite. After three weeks in this condition, the doctors advised that he had but two or three days to live. They suggested he return to Uganda to die.

His physician did not give up. As Head of the Cancer Institute, he was aware of orthodox cancer treatments. He was also aware that they all had failed Odongo. Yet, he continually searched for the answer to cure his patient and good friend. He thought when he found the answer he was looking for, it would help all mankind.

He heard about a dietary cancer treatment that proved successful in 25 terminal cancer cases in Dallas, Texas. John Richardson, M.D. of California, developed the remedy. He flew to Dallas to gather the proper ingredients for the remedy, hoping to help save Odongo.

He mixed Richardson's cancer treatment into a mush, which he administered through a tube attached to Odongo's stomach. In less than 24 hours, Odongo responded. He began to improve. He was given enemas and herbal laxatives to keep his bowels open, and high doses of vitamin C beginning with 12 (twelve) grams a day (50% ascorbic acid powder and 50% calcium ascorbate powder) administered to help flush away his high toxic levels.

Within two weeks, Odongo's head returned to normal size. X-rays disclosed the cancer in both lungs had completely disappeared. The tumor in his brain had not yet changed, but Odongo spoke for the first time in seven months. He complained about the hospital food, a good sign.

Odongo's physician gave him personal daily care, paying close attention to each detail of the Richardson Dietary Program. He ground all the vitamin and mineral tablets into powdered form to be administered through the stomach tube. He continually checked all vital signs, charting the improving condition of his terminally-ill patient. He read and absorbed everything he could concerning the dietary treatment of cancer, consulting daily with the nutritionist who first provided him with the Richardson Diet. Odongo's physician developed a profound respect for the healing powers of natural medicine.

Why this dramatic reversal in General Odongo's terminal condition? Since the primary cause of cancer is toxicity, Dr. Richardson's Diet was effective because of its ability to remove toxins from the body. Attention to the detail of two to three bowel movements a day was essential (an important way to eliminate the toxins). Twice during Odongo's recovery, he became constipated for several days, resulting in swelling and unconsciousness.

With enemas working and doses up to 40 (forty) grams of sodium ascorbate per day, the resulting diarrhea gave rise to detoxification, which brought Odongo back to consciousness and to improved health.

Odongo's physician enthusiastically (and quite naively) told doctors at the hospital what he was doing. They politely advised him that he would have to practice his "witchcraft" elsewhere - not in *their* hospital. He knew he could not move Odongo from the hospital at this stage, so he administered his nutritional cure when the doctors were not looking. He poured the pharmaceuticals down the toilet.

In a matter of a few short weeks, Odongo and his physician returned
to Uganda. Odongo lived for six months beyond his predicted death.
In his final months, he felt less pain and a return of human dignity.
He lived a modest extension of life with upgraded quality.

OVARIAN CANCER

In her sixties, Dr. Todd was a practicing psychologist. She withdrew
from practice when her abdominal problem was diagnosed as a rapidly spreading cancer of the ovary. Her abdomen had swelled consid-
erably. A CAT scan revealed a massive tumor with tentacles spreading
in every direction; obviously inoperable and apparently "terminal."
None of the cancer was removed except samples for biopsy, revealing
the origin of the cancer in an ovary.

Her oncologist insisted she take a round of chemotherapy, namely
cis platinum. He was so insistent, she agreed. At the same time, she
became aware of detoxification and nutritional programs, which she
began immediately.

Dr. Todd suffered *greatly* during the injection of cis platinum. Her
physician had not fully prepared her for its toxicity. The nurse
informed her to be very, very still during the intravenous drip injection, for if she were to knock the needle from her arm, the drug could
immediately destroy her skin. Dr. Todd wondered what the drug was
doing to her internally.

After the injection, she experienced memory loss, attributing this to
damage to her brain cells. She refused any further chemotherapy,
but continued to religiously follow the detoxification and nutritional
supplement program. On her own, she increased her dosage of sele-
nium to one (1) mg. daily (200 - 400 mcg. is the average dose). Published evidence shows this dosage not to be toxic, but should not be
exceeded past this amount. She did have a problem with high dosages
of vitamin C, however. A suspected allergy to the corn from which
the vitamin was derived was suspected. She switched to vitamin C

made from Sago palm, experiencing no further allergic symptoms at twenty (20) grams daily.

Dr. Todd had problems with her colon all her adult life, experiencing considerable constipation and painful gas. This contributed to her high toxic load by causing conditions allowing the malignancy to grow.

Ninety days after diagnosis, the cis platinum injection, and the start of the nutritional diet, she went in for another CAT scan. It was negative! Such extraordinary reversal needs further explanation.

BURKITT'S CANCER DISCOVERY

Dennis Burkitt, M.D. of London, England, for whom Burkitt's Lymphoma is named, is one of the world's most outstanding cancer specialists in medical history. Most of his work was done in Africa. In one of his publications, he reported on a group of American oncologists who visited his hospital in Africa. They left a large supply of chemotherapeutic drugs and instructions for use. Dr. Burkitt reported that for the first few years, all his efforts in treating cancer with the drugs ended in the death of his patients with one exception. A young African man was so frightened of the drugs, he ran away from the hospital after his first injection. He lived in the bush. Several years later, some of the hospital personnel recognized him, reporting he was alive and well.

From this one survivor, Dr. Burkitt concluded that American drugs did have anticancer effects by stimulating the body's immune system, but the Americans did not yet know how to use them properly. They were guilty of overkill, of making doses too large, in giving too many dosages, eventually destroying the body's immune system and ability to heal itself from that point forward. From then on, Dr. Burkitt gave no more than one or two injections of a low dosage, just enough to stimulate the immune system. He then began witnessing recoveries from his cancer patients.

Dr. Burkitt was right. There is never a need to "kill" every last cancer cell. This is impossible, anyway. Many cancer researchers believe we are all born with potential cancer cells in our bodies which are only able to grow and manifest as tumors when oxygen levels are low due to high levels of toxicity in the body, or when the immune system is impaired.

Whether the platinum alone, or solely the diet, or a combination of the two performed the trick is merely academic. When fighting cancer or any degenerative disease, I recommend the "shot gun approach." Research everything possible as a sensible treatment alternative, and something should work for you. If you can decipher which curative method or methods were responsible for your healing success, that's even better so you will know for sure what to attribute it to. But if it's hard to determine if one or a combination of many healing methods were responsible for your healing, then so be it. At least you healed and have a plan to help others!

Perhaps the one dose of cis platinum stimulated Dr. Todd's immune system. Aided by the detoxification and nutritional program, her cancer reversed itself.

Nutritional Background
For Detoxing Cancer

In general, all cancer patients do better if they eliminate red meat during the recovery period. Many cancer patients, probably the majority, have impaired digestion due to either a lack of hydrochloric acid in the stomach or a lack of pancreatic digestive enzymes. Both are needed for the proper digestion of meat. If either is lacking, undigested or incompletely digested protein is picked up by the blood, adding toxicity to the body. Undigested proteins is highly toxic.

Properly digested protein is not susceptible to anaerobic or putrefied bacteria. Nonetheless, undigested protein is readily attacked by disease-producing bacteria, creating a series of toxic breakdown byproducts, some of which are picked up by the blood and add to the toxic load in the already diseased body.

There is evidence that all the pancreatic proteolytic (protein-digesting) enzyme output is used up in the digestion of protein. None remains to circulate throughout the body where these enzymes can encounter and digest malignant cells or the "shell" the body builds around the cells.

THE SIGNIFICANCE OF
VITAMIN C AND CANCER

The benefits of vitamin C in the battle against cancer are many. This vitamin has been called the body's greatest detoxifier. It combines with the toxins in the body, cleanses them, and reduces the total toxic load the body is carrying.

Normal cells combine oxygen with fuel from food in a "burning" process to derive heat and energy. The higher the oxygen level, the greater the vitality. The malignant cell, on the other hand, has a different method of respiration called "fermentation," which takes place only when the oxygen level is low or absent. Therefore, the tissue in which a cancer is growing is low in oxygen, or the toxic load in that tissue has stalled the oxygenating reactions. When the body is detoxified, the oxygen levels in the body rise and the oxygenating reactions resume. The conditions under which the malignant cell proliferates are now gone. Normal cell function takes over and the cancer cell dies in the presence of oxygen. The dead cancer cell is then excreted through the normal organs of elimination.

Early nutritionist William Cathcart, M.D. refined the method of detoxification with mega doses of vitamin C. He recommended increasing the vitamin C level to bowel tolerance, the point at which the body tissues are saturated with vitamin C. Beyond this point, diarrhea results.

An optimal way to detoxify is to begin supplementing two to three (2-3) grams of vitamin C the first day and increase by one (1) gram each day until a liquid stool develops. At this point, cut the daily intake by one (1) gram (1,000 mg.). Remain at this level until another liquid stool develops. Then, cut back another one (1) gram. As the body's toxic load is reduced and the body's need for vitamin C is reduced, the body will tolerate less and less.

By using this method, the average daily dosage should remain around four to six (4-6) grams per day while staying at or near tissue saturation. The colon will also be cleansed of any impacted fecal matter without any colonics or enemas.

A twelve (12) gram/per day range for a 150-pound human fits well with animal studies. Vitamin C is normal to the body. As mentioned on page 39, all animals make vitamin C in their livers with the exception of the guinea pig, the monkey, the ape, a species of bat in India, and humans. A 150-pound animal makes on the average thirteen (13) grams of vitamin C per day. However, if it is placed under stress, its output is greatly increased. Up to 100 grams/per day have been measured in animals under severe stress. No matter the cause, psychological, excessive cold or heat, an infectious agent, a drug, a poison, or electric shock, all will deplete vitamin C levels in the body and greatly increase the need for more. Hospitals administering high drug levels to patients, or patients who have undergone operations, radiation, or other stressful medical procedures, are the best candidates for vitamin C.

DOUBLE RECOVERY FROM METASTASIZED LUNG CANCER

Claude is a 77-year-old man diagnosed with "terminal" cancer in both lungs. It had spread to his liver. It had also eaten a hole in his neck bone, and he was wearing a neck brace. His oncologist said nothing could be done except chemotherapy, yet in his opinion, it would be of little to no benefit.

Upon learning about the remarkable results of vitamin C in "acute" cancer patients in Loch Lomondside, Scotland reported by Linus Pauling, PhD. and Swan Cameron, M.D., Claude began taking the same dose used by Dr. Cameron's patients, ten (10) grams of the vitamin per day.

His checkup after 90 days revealed the neck bone was healing and recalcifying. The other two cancer sites remained unchanged.

After six months, his checkup disclosed that his neck brace was no longer needed as the neck bone had completely healed. More importantly, the other two sites showed substantial regression of the cancer. After nine months, a routine checkup disclosed no signs of cancer. This case certainly confirmed the findings made by Drs. Pauling and Cameron.

A couple of months later, while still taking ten (10) grams of vitamin C each day, Claude began developing lung problems. He was admitted to the hospital and tests disclosed lung congestion and fluid accumulation. Cancer cells were detected in the fluid drained from his lungs. His oncologist offered no hope.

For the second time, Claude restored his health as once before, so he knew what to do. He searched, again, for the source of his cancer with hopes of eliminating recurring exposure to the cancer-forming toxin, and increased his vitamin C and nutrient levels to assist in removing another layer of cancer cells.

VANISHING SKIN CANCER

Lori wanted to know if there was anything nutritional that would heal the black mole growing rapidly on her left thigh. It had a gray furry coating on it and was about the size of a dime. She did not want a scar from surgical removal, but confessed her dermatologist wanted to cut it off, along with several other moles he was concerned about. A biopsy showed the growth to be pre-cancerous.

Written in the book <u>Vitamin C and Cancer</u> by H.L.Newbold, M.D., excellent results were obtained in drying up skin cancers using a 50/50 mixture of sodium ascorbate powder and a vanishing cream made of aloe vera, H2O2, glycerin, and olive oil. She decided to try it, and applied the mixture topically every night, covering it with a bandage.

At the end of one week, there was noticeable reduction in size, and the gray furry coating disappeared. In three weeks, the growth had vanished, leaving no trace of where it had been. After three months, Lori returned to her doctor who couldn't find the growth. She continues to use the *10 Step Detoxification Program* along with her nutritional program and cream when needed to keep her blood and skin clear of any pre-cancerous growths.

LYMPHOMA

Mike developed nodules on his arms and shoulders. One was excised for biopsy. The resulting report of lymphoma alarmed him. He began the *10 Step Detoxification Program* after he had a hair analysis done, and followed his nutritional program religiously for five months, averaging thirty (30) grams of vitamin C per day.

During this time period, his malignancy slowly decreased with merely a few new nodules remaining swollen under his arms. The lymph nodes in his groin area returned to their normal size within a matter of weeks. He reviewed and readjusted his nutritional diet several times during his recovery period to stay ahead of any changes, but everything appeared to be steadily working effectively. The advance of the disease seemed to be slowing down.

Mike did agree to have some radiation. This helped him some; his skin became quite irritated, red, and flaky. He administered interferon injections himself, but it did not seem to help as much as it caused nausea and body pain. All the while, he continued to follow his nutritional program. He completely lost his sense of taste and smell and had little appetite prior to getting on the nutritional program. As his nodules shrank in size, it became apparent the nutritional program was working along with the medicine he was taking.

Once a month, Mike met with a group of cancer patients also on the *10 Step Detoxification Program* who, using nutrition, had previously recovered, or were currently recovering, from cancer. One of them suggested he add vitamin B17 tablets to his dietary detoxification regimen.

Mike began taking six vitamin B17 tablets per day. On the second day, his depression and weakness vanished. His sense of taste and appetite returned. The smile on his face was a joy to behold when he returned several weeks later to report that a checkup by his physician disclosed his cancerous nodules had definitely receded. His doctors were amazed at his recovery progress.

The significance of this case is that, whereas the *Detoxification Program* is sufficient for most cancer cases, some cases need the added anti-cancer effects of vitamin B17 and low-dose pharmaceuticals to gain control of the disease. Let us not forget Dr. Burkitt's philosophy that administering cancer drugs may have value when accompanied by nutritional alternatives. One, both, or the combination of all methods may be the reason some cancer patients survive and go on to live a cancer-free and drug-free life. Mike used all the tools available to him in moderation and healed from Stage IV lymphoma cancer.

BREAST CANCER FROM HORMONES

Jackie's lump in her right breast naturally concerned her. She went to her doctor who performed a needle biopsy, which confirmed the presence of malignant cells. A mastectomy and radiation were performed. A few weeks later, another lump appeared in the same area. A second needle biopsy was again positive. She was aware that the needle (biopsy) could spread the disease by leaking malignant cells through the puncture made by the needle into the tumor. At this point, she rejected any further surgery or radiation, believing they had failed her.

The *10 Step Detoxification Program* was explained to her, along with the possibility that her cancer was estrogen dependent, induced by excess estrogen in the body. The excess estrogen build up was not so much from high production of the hormone, but from the inability to properly detoxify the excess. After following the *Detoxification Program* for four weeks, the second cancerous lump was no longer present; having been detoxified and reabsorbed by the body, then eliminated through the normal channels of excretion.

One year later, another lump appeared at the same site as the first lump, near the scar from her operation. She admitted she had not been following her nutritional program over the past three months. Back on the program, her lump disappeared in less than three weeks. She remained cancer free for almost one year.

Then, she developed a painful tooth. She ignored it for as long as she could withstand it. After several weeks of suffering, her dentist extracted the tooth, giving her painkillers, anesthetics, and antibiotics.

Within two days, another lump appeared in her breast, but not in the usual place. In this instance, it appeared adjacent to the right collarbone approximately three inches below the site of the abscessed tooth.

She increased the detoxification supplements, including twenty (20) grams of vitamin C per day. Her lump had diminished, so she canceled the scheduled surgery. In a few days, the lump was gone. She then reduced her vitamin C intake to the maintenance level of ten (10) grams spread throughout the day.

The Boy Whose House Nearly Killed Him

"TERMINAL" CANCER INDUCED BY TERMITE PESTICIDE

The story of the Bergens was published in the Sunday Supplement of the Dallas Morning News in the late 1970s. The article was summarized as follows: Mr. and Dr. Bergen purchased their "dream" house in an upper-class neighborhood in Dallas, Texas. Shortly after moving in, they and their two children became ill. One of their sons became very sick. Tests disclosed a rare form of cancer lying against his liver. It was successfully removed by an operation. Tests run by his doctors revealed high levels of chlorinated hydrocarbons in his body tissues.

Toxicologists from two universities separately examined what turned out to be their "nightmare" house. The tests run by these poison experts revealed that the house and everything in it were too highly contaminated for human inhabitants. The Bergens learned that the same major pesticide company had sprayed the house six times in the previous year. The Bergens left everything in the house and moved out. They filed lawsuits against the pesticide company, the previous owner, and the real estate company.

After several months, the Bergen's problems worsened. The boy's cancer returned. This time it was wrapped around the aorta of the heart. Operations involving the aorta have a 98 percent rate of failure and death. His physicians recommended no further course of treatment. His mother grew extremely worried after the doctor's explained the cancer could eat through the aorta in perhaps two to three weeks, resulting in the death of her child.

She immediately sought help elsewhere. She took her 12-year-old son to John Richardson, M.D. in Reno, Nevada, who placed the boy on the diet documented in his book, <u>Vitamin B17 Case Histories</u>. Upon returning to Dallas, she visited a nutritionist, the late Steve Fuqua, to talk about her son. By adding the following, she modified her son's dietary program:

1. One (1) Coenzyme Q tablet by Organik® to raise the oxygenating enzymes in the body.
2. Vitamin A levels temporarily increased to 100,000 units. Hundreds of papers have been published on the anti-cancer effect of this vitamin.
3. One (1) cup of yogurt daily.
4. Two (2) garlic capsules per meal for detoxification.
5. An amino acid supplement, with one (1) gram extra L-Cystein mid-morning and one (1) gram mid-afternoon for detoxification.
6. 500 mg. zinc orotate daily. Hans Nieper, M.D. of Hanover, West Germany reports excellent results using this nutrient in his extensive European practice.
7. Vitamin C, beginning with twelve (12) grams spread throughout the day, increasing three (3) grams each day, titrating up to bowel tolerance, per William Cathcart, M.D. Then, cutting back three (3) grams following diarrhea. Fifty percent (50%) calcium ascorbate and fifty percent (50%) ascorbic acid were used.

Young Bergen topped out at thirty-three (33) grams of vitamin C per day, at which level he saturated his tissues with the vitamin C for the first time. Excess vitamin C was rejected, indicated by development of a loose stool. Using this method of cutting the vitamin C intake by three (3) grams every time diarrhea developed, allowed him to taper down to eight (8) grams daily. His ability to accept a high dosage meant he had been severely toxic.

Thirty days after beginning the modified Richardson Diet, another scan was performed. His doctors were astounded to find the cancer had vanished. Even more amazing to his parents, none of the physicians showed the slightest interest in how this young boy performed this "miracle" of healing himself.

Other inferences of this case:
1. Detoxification is rapid using the above program monitored by a certified nutritionist.
2. Healing is quick when the proper conditions are attained in the body, especially with children.
3. The body has amazing capacity to heal itself when treated properly.

A PERSONAL TESTIMONY

For 29 years, I was the epitome of good health. I was leading an active life, jogging four miles a day, and enjoying an exciting career in real estate development. Then came an abrupt change. On November 1, 1982, I found myself being prepped for brain surgery, only to have a highly malignant tumor removed. After surgery, the neurosurgeon felt I had, at best, six months to live -- a textbook case of terminal cancer. Fortunately, the textbooks aren't always correct.

Over the next 10 days while in the hospital recovering from the surgery, I began researching everything I could find about this new disease I had. The technical name for my type of cancer was Glio-Blastoma-Multiformee, level IV, supposedly one of the more severe forms of cancer and highly malignant. In the first visit after the operation with the doctor, he indicated the tumor he removed was about the size of an orange. I probably should have asked whether he was referring to a naval or mandarin orange, but at that point, I was sufficiently impressed that what was in my head was very serious.

While I was fully aware of the reality of the disease I had contracted, the normal anxiety usually associated with such a life-threatening disease was completely absent from my emotions. Having been a born-again Christian for many years, I attest to the fact that God can fully heal any emotional burden and provide a "peace that passes all human understanding." In the Bible, Philippines 4:6-7, God describes how you can have your heart and your mind guarded from anxiety. It is a simple process of finding *personal* peace through a *personal* relationship. Five years after my surgery, I can confidently say that God still heals people in the 20th century.

While in the hospital, several close friends inquired as to any knowledge I had about nutrition and cancer. I was just beginning to learn about all the issues that affect cancer, but had not come across any information regarding the diet and cancer. My friends proceeded to tell me there was a very definite link between what we eat and the incidence of cancer. They began to describe several types of diets that had a strong curative effect in dealing with cancer. Examining further these recommended nutritional programs, specifically macrobiotics and a vegetarian diet, my husband and I began to explore similar, related programs such as the Kelly Approach, Metabolic Biology, several Oriental diets, and finally, the Richardson Program. As we studied these various programs in greater detail, there appeared to be a common thread among them: the elimination of red meats, alcoholic beverages, tobacco products, and the wide array of preservatives, food additives, and artificial sweeteners and colorings.

After a lot of thought and prayer, I decided to pursue the Richardson Program. This program was basically a lacto-vegetarian diet that included a large amount of vitamin supplements and herbs on a regular basis. I would have to say that the adjustment to this new diet was more of an excruciating ordeal than the entire revelation of the disease and the actual surgery. Gone were some of my favorite foods: hamburgers, BLT sandwiches, steaks, hot dogs, ice cream, etc. If I had been dealing with a broken leg or just a minor health problem and was told to pursue this diet for complete health, I doubt I would have had the discipline to stick with it. However, dealing with a life-threatening disease with a six-month life expectancy -- I felt it was "battle stations," -- and made a total commitment to pursue the program.

As I discussed this new nutritional program with the physicians involved in my case, I was confronted with immediate rejection of any possible merits toward a nutritional program in terms of dealing with cancer. The frustration of the complete lack of support from the medical practitioners, coupled with the difficulty of giving up all the "good foods" I had grown accustomed to made sticking with this program most difficult. However, the human body is designed to break old habits with repetitive frequency of different behavioral patterns. Eating habits are no different. As time marched on, the new diet became more and more comfortable.

One of the major concerns I had as I began adjusting my diet was the issue of energy -- with the elimination of meats, would I be able to maintain an active lifestyle. Within six months of the initial surgery, I was involved in all the previous activities I had been active in before the cancer ordeal. I returned to jogging on a daily basis, was actively involved in various sports activities, and 15 months after the surgery, conceived my fourth child.

In the five years following my surgery, it has been interesting to observe the doctors' reactions to my victory over cancer. At my six-month check up, upon reviewing the most recent CAT scan of the area previously infested by the cancer, the neurosurgeon thought we were experiencing a miracle. At the nine-month visit, he stated the cancer that surrounded the tumor following surgery had shown absolutely no sign of any growth or advancement. At the first year anniversary, he indicated if conditions did not change after, probably, the third year, the cancer situation could be declared in remission. It was about this time that he began to inquire more into the nutritional approach I had pursued, requesting a copy of the actual diet program I was on. After a clean bill of health on my 18-month visit, he referred me to a patient who had a brain tumor very similar to mine. He later relayed that my progress had convinced him there must be some benefit to the nutritional approach.

On the two-year anniversary, the CAT scan revealed there was absolutely no sign of cancer and the only evidence of what happened 24 months ago was scar tissue where the initial tumor had been removed. At that point, the neurosurgeon uttered the magic words, "your previous cancer is in full remission!" -- a strong indication that textbook statistics are not always correct.

Every year on the anniversary of my initial surgery, I go in for a checkup, which has been an annual affirmation of my good health. Along the way, I have studied and researched everything I can get my hands on relative to cancer and nutrition. Several years ago, I came across an organization, The American Institute for Cancer Research, which focuses completely on the correlation between cancer and nutrition. This institute is a medically based research group totally focused on studying how the diet can be a curative and preventative measure against the disease of cancer.

This organization produces a free quarterly newsletter. It can be obtained by writing: The American Institute for Cancer Research, 500 North Washington Street, Falls Church, Virginia 22046.

In the course of leading an active and vibrant life, I come across many people in the initial throws of cancer. As I share my experiences, many people feel I am a living miracle. Others think the reason for my good health is a direct result of the nutritional program. I simply praise the Lord for His healing powers and continue a diet that enhances my long-run health and gives me the best assurance of avoiding a future recurrence of the dreaded disease of cancer.

Endometriosis

Emma is a very vivacious schoolteacher in her early thirties. Recently married, she and her husband want children. Emma developed pains associated with her lower abdomen. A thorough medical exam disclosed endometrial tissue from the lining of the uterus growing in several areas outside the womb.

The diagnosis of endometriosis was apparent, and her physicians recommended an operation to remove the offending growths. Emma didn't relish the idea of an operation and the resulting scars. Knowing there was another way, she agreed to give her body a chance to heal itself. The body has amazing capacity to do so if treated properly. She was asked the standard questions about her diet and what supplements she took, if any. Her hair was cut for a hair mineral test. The elements of a good diet were explained to her, and it was pointed out that endometriosis had certain similarities to cancer, and the *10 Step Detoxification Program* was an excellent program for her to follow.

Cancer can be the result of the trophoblast cells growing in the wrong places in the body. In her case, endometrial tissue was growing in the wrong place in her body. This implied her immune system was impaired and that she was toxic. Her immune system was perhaps unable to recognize the endometrial growths as foreign and/or unable to mount an inflammatory reaction necessary to eliminate them, similar to a cancer patient. Her impaired immune system implied severe dietary deficiencies and/or a very high toxic load.

It was recommended she begin taking vitamin C daily, increasing by one (1) gram each day until she developed diarrhea or a liquid stool. Her upper limit was thirty-three (33) grams daily, quite high for a person weighing 110 pounds. This indicated a very high toxic load.

Her hair mineral test results showed eight (8) minerals to be very low, seven (7) toxic metals above 90 percent tissue saturation, and an indication she had a hydrochloric acid deficiency within her stomach. This acid deficiency can predispose humans to cancer because of the inability to properly perform the first step of protein digestion in the stomach. Undigested food proteins absorbed into the body raises the toxic load the body is carrying, thus impairing the immune system and creating conditions under which both cancer and endometriosis can occur.

Emma followed the *10 Step Detoxification Program* along with specific nutritional recommendations, and took the supplements indicated by the hair mineral test. Within one month, all her abdominal pain had subsided. The operation was forgotten.

She asked, "When can I start raising children?" Emma was told she definitely should not get pregnant until the results of her second hair analysis (six months after the first one) showed normal. She agreed. During a check up five months after beginning her nutritional program, her physician used a device to look inside the abdominal cavity. He reported no endometriosis, only some scar tissue at the former sites.

CANCER OF THE PROSTATE

David is a petroleum engineer. He never stopped to think that the many chemicals he is exposed to could be toxic or carcinogenic.

At age 62, he developed a hard knot on his prostate and had it checked. The biopsy came back cancerous. A scan revealed that metastasis had occurred to the surrounding lymph nodes. David elected to do the dietary program and refused radiation suggested by his doctor. His physician offered little hope of a complete recovery, even with radiation.

David religiously followed the *10 Step Detoxification Program*. After one week, he called to report his skin was giving off a very strong odor. He smelled like petrochemicals. Three showers a day and different deodorants did not stop the odor. He called to ask about the cause of his horrible body odor. "Could this be the toxic chemicals coming out of my body?" Yes.

This very strong odor continued for several weeks. Heavy smokers with lung cancer frequently have an odor of stale smoke during detoxification.

David topped out at sixty (60) grams of vitamin C per day. He gradually decreased the dosage to thirty (30) grams per day, which was the daily dose he needed to regularly prevent the high toxic load from redeveloping, and possibly predisposing him to cancer. He has remained at this level and, of course, cancer free for over three years.

FIRST-PERSON CASE HISTORY

This is the case history of a 49-year-old registered nurse, written by the patient.

Pt. is gravida VII, para V. Postoperative diagnosis:
- Left adnexal mass: poorly differentiated adenocarcinoma.
- Right ovary: poorly differentiated adenocarcinoma.
- Left fallopian tube: hydrosalpinx.
- Left ovary: lumeinized cystic follicles.
- Right fallopian tube: no pathological diagnosis.
- Uterus endometrium: cystic and adenomatous hyperplasia with focal well-differentiated adenocarcinoma.
- Myometrium: leiomyoma.
- Cervix: no pathological diagnosis.

After surgery, I was referred to an OB/GYN Oncologist. His recommendations:
1. Chemotherapy followed by an exploratory laporotomy.
2. Ten months post-op to see if "any cancer cells were still hiding."
3. The numerous side effects of chemotherapy were read to me.

4. Drugs would be given to offset nausea and vomiting, and I would be hospitalized for chemotherapy treatments.

I asked what the prognosis would be without chemotherapy. The answer: possibly six months to live.

I chose not to follow the oncologist's recommendations. I had multiple undiagnosed breast masses and a large, painless mass on the lower left extremity, mid-tibia, undiagnosed.

Ten days post-op, I chose to try nutritional therapy. Adhering strictly to a nutritional program as well as taking supplements, I started with 18 (eighteen) grams/day of vitamin C, becoming saturated at 60 (sixty) grams/day. Being in the medical profession, I was ridiculed and harassed continually for my unorthodox decision.

Two years post-op, I was alive and well. I had no adverse side effects, and continued working full time as a nurse. There was no evidence of carcinoma. The breast masses and leg mass were no longer obvious. Those in the medical profession who ridiculed me now call my diagnosis a mistake, or they ask me for further information about my results.

It should be noted that:
1. I strictly adhered to my diet.
2. I took my vitamin supplements exactly as recommended.

Resources and Further Reading

About Dr. Hull:
http://www.janethull.com/about/

Contact Dr. Hull:
http://www.janethull.com/contact.php

Dr. Hull's Free Monthly Newsletter:
http://www.healthynewsletter.com/

PRODUCTS AND SERVICES

Information About The Richardson Cancer Prevention Diet:
http://www.alternativecancerdiet.com/

SweetPoison – Dr. Hull's Aspartame Experience:
http://www.sweetpoison.com/

Splenda®: Is It Safe Or Not?:
http://www.issplendasafe.com/
http://www.splendaexposed.com/

Dr. Hull's Vitamins and Supplements:
http://www.janethull.com/vitamins

10 Step Detoxification Program and Kit:
http://www.detoxprogram.net/

Hair Analysis Testing:
http://www.hairanalysisprogram.com/

pH Balance Test Kit:
http://www.janethull.com/ph-balance-testing/

CANCER RESOURCES

Guide To Alternative Cancer Treatments:
http://www.alternative-cancer.net/

Cure Your Cancer:
http://www.getandstaywell.com/

Alternative Therapy Cancer Guide:
http://www.cancerguide.org/alternative.html

Alternative Cancer Therapies & Clinics:
http://www.cancure.org/

Center For Complementary and Alternative Medicine:
http://nccam.nih.gov/